Places In Time
A Kid's Historic Guide to the Changing Names and Places of the World

A Brief Political and Geographic History of

Latin America

Where Are . . . Gran Colombia, La Plata, and Dutch Guiana

Mitchell Lane
PUBLISHERS

P.O. Box 196
Hockessin, Delaware 19707
Visit us on the web: www.mitchelllane.com
Comments? email us: mitchelllane@mitchelllane.com

Places In Time
A Kid's Historic Guide to the Changing Names and Places of the World

Titles in the Series

A Brief Political and Geographic History of . . .

Africa
Where Are Belgian Congo, Rhodesia, and Kush?

Asia
Where Are Saigon, Kampuchea, and Burma?

Europe
Where Are Prussia, Gaul, and the Holy Roman Empire?

Latin America
Where Are Gran Columbia, La Plata, and Dutch Guiana?

The Middle East
Where Are Persia, Babylon, and the Ottoman Empire?

North America
Where Are New France, New Netherland, and New Sweden?

Places In Time

A Kid's Historic Guide to the Changing Names and Places of the World

A Brief Political and
Geographic History of

Latin
America

Where Are···Gran Colombia, La Plata, and Dutch Guiana

Earle Rice Jr.

Mitchell Lane
PUBLISHERS

P.O. Box 196
Hockessin, Delaware 19707
Visit us on the web: www.mitchelllane.com
Comments? email us: mitchelllane@mitchelllane.com

Copyright © 2008 by Mitchell Lane Publishers. All rights reserved. No part of this book may be reproduced without written permission from the publisher. Printed and bound in the United States of America.

Printing   1   2   3   4   5   6   7   8   9

Library of Congress Cataloging-in-Publication Data
Rice, Earle.
    A brief political and geographic history of Latin America: where are Gran Colombia, La Plata, and Dutch Guiana? / by Earle Rice Jr.
        p. cm. — (Places in time)
    Includes bibliographical references and index.
    ISBN-13: 978-1-58415-626-0 (library bound)
    1. Latin America—History—Juvenile literature. 2. Latin America—Historical geography—Juvenile literature. I. Title.
F1410.R396 2007
980—dc22
                                                                            2007000781

PHOTO CREDITS: Maps by Jonathan Scott—pp. 6, 7, 8, 18, 30, 32, 39, 42, 50, 55, 62, 71, 74, 81, 86; p. 10—Alejo Fernández/photo by Manuel Rosa; pp. 11, 16, 48, 54, 90, 94—Barbara Marvis; pp. 12, 25—Library of Congress; p. 14—Dietrich Bartel/Creative Commons; p. 15—Paul V. Galvin Library/Digital History Collection; pp. 21, 36, 54, 59, 67—JupiterImages; p. 23—Superstock; p. 26—Museo Napoleonico; p. 27—Palacio Nacional; p. 33—Biblioteca Nacional Library; p. 38—Cándido Lopez; p. 40—Brazilian Government; p. 44—Uffizi Gallery; p. 45—Valter Campanato, Agência Brasil; p. 46—Gold Museum/Bogotá, Colombia; p. 47—National Portrait Gallery, London; p. 52—University of North Carolina, Pembroke; p. 57—J.M. Moreau Jr./P. Duflos Junior; p. 58—The Granger Collection, New York; p. 60—Florida Center for Instructional Technology; p. 66—Arturo Michelena/Galería de Arte Nacional; p. 70—J. V. Cañarete/National Museum of Bogotá, Colombia; p. 72—John Carter Brown Library; p. 76—North Wind Picture Archives; p. 79—Three Lions/Getty Images; p. 80—Hart Preston/Time Life Pictures/Getty Images; pp. 83, 84—AFP/Getty Images; p. 89—NASA; p. 92—Pedro de Subercaseaux/Museo Nacional de Bellas Artes, Buenos Aires; p. 93—Juan Mauricio Rugendas; p. 95—Government of Chile; p. 96—Keystone/Getty Images.

PUBLISHER'S NOTE: This story is based on the author's extensive research, which he believes to be accurate. Documentation of such research is contained on page 90.
    The maps created for these books have been thoroughly researched by our authors, who have extensive backgrounds in world history. Every effort has been made to represent close approximations to these places in time.
    The internet sites referenced herein were active as of the publication date. Due to the fleeting nature of some web sites, we cannot guarantee they will all be active when you are reading this book.
    To reflect current usage, we have chosen to use the secular era designations BCE ("before the common era") and CE ("of the common era") instead of the traditional designations BC ("before Christ") and AD (*anno Domini,* "in the year of the Lord").
                                                                                    PLB

Places In Time

Table of Contents

PRESENT-DAY LATIN AMERICA

Latin America includes all of the Americas south of the United States of America. The numbers on the map indicate the chapter in which each area is dicussed.

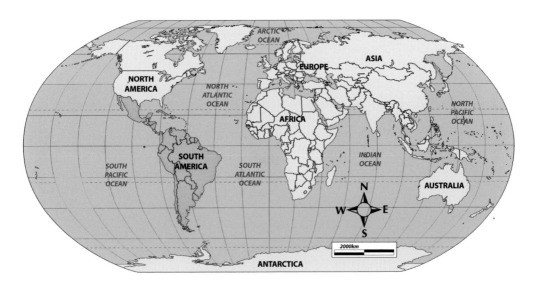

Gran Colombia, La Plata, and Dutch Guiana · Where Are...

Introduction

Nothing under the sun remains the same. Everything changes over time. Cities, states, nations, governments, and the world itself all change in due course. Change occurs for many reasons, both natural and human caused, some good and some not so good. Winter snows create gushing streams of sparkling clear water in the spring. Over time, azure skies over industrial areas turn ashen with smog. Change is inevitable, sometimes welcome, sometimes not. In either case, change is often confusing—particularly when it affects places in time.

In the eight chapters that follow, we will journey south of the United States border, sail the Spanish Main, and fly down to Rio on a whirlwind tour of the places and politics of times past. When we return, everyone will know the answer to our theme question: "Where are Gran Colombia, La Plata, and Dutch Guiana?"—and a whole lot more. The numbers on the map to the left correspond to the area featured in the chapter with the same number.

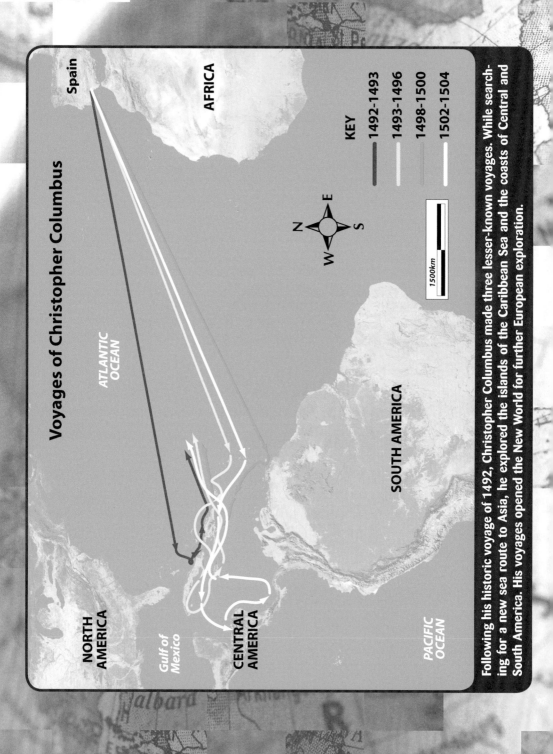

Voyages of Christopher Columbus

Spain

AFRICA

NORTH AMERICA

ATLANTIC OCEAN

Gulf of Mexico

CENTRAL AMERICA

SOUTH AMERICA

PACIFIC OCEAN

N
W E
S

1500km

KEY

1492–1493
1493–1496
1498–1500
1502–1504

Following his historic voyage of 1492, Christopher Columbus made three lesser-known voyages. While search-ing for a new sea route to Asia, he explored the islands of the Caribbean Sea and the coasts of Central and South America. His voyages opened the New World for further European exploration.

Mundus Novus: Opening the New World

Christopher Columbus called his grand scheme the "Enterprise of the Indies." Simply put, it was a plan to reach the Orient by sailing west from Europe. He sought a direct route to the Indies and the fabled island of Cipango (now Japan). His inspiration came largely from reading the *Travels of Marco Polo*. Polo was an Italian explorer who had journeyed across Asia to Cathay (China) about two centuries earlier. His account of his twenty-four-year journey told of fabulous cities and enormous riches in the Far East.

Columbus first conceived the notion for his "Enterprise" in 1484. Four years later, Portuguese navigator Bartolomeu Dias sailed south along the west coast of Africa. His discovery of Africa's Cape of Good Hope opened the door to the first sea route to Cipango and its riches—spices, silks, gold, silver, precious gems, and much more. But it was a long and dangerous route. Columbus believed a shorter, safer path to the Far East and the Indies lay to the west. He spent the next eight years seeking support for his westward voyage. Spanish monarchs Ferdinand V and Isabella I finally agreed to fund it.

On August 3, 1492, three small ships scudded down the Río Tinto from Palos, Spain, on the morning ebb and cleaved smartly into the open sea. Columbus set a course for the Canary Islands, which lie about 800 miles off the northwest coast of Africa. His tiny fleet consisted of his flagship, the *Santa Maria*, a three-masted, square-rigged cargo vessel, and two caravels—smaller trading vessels—the *Pinta* and the *Niña*. Together, they carried ninety men. The fleet underwent

Genoese navigator and explorer Christopher Columbus sailed west to find a new sea route to the Orient. Instead, he found a New World. He is celebrated as the discoverer of America.

repairs and took on supplies in the Canaries. On September 6, the three ships put out to sea again, this time striking a west-southwest course to take advantage of the following trade winds. The greatest voyage of discovery in human history had begun.

Columbus had estimated the distance between the Canaries and the Indies at some 2,400 nautical miles. (A nautical mile equals 1.15 land miles.) He predicted that he could cover the distance in twenty-one days. But the actual distance from the Canaries to the Indies is roughly 10,600 nautical miles. Thus, both his distance and time estimates fell uncomfortably short of reality. Thirty days passed in an unknown sea with no land in sight. The crews aboard all three ships started to stir restlessly. To calm their fears, Columbus lied to them about the distance traveled each day. Several more days passed, but no land came into view. Columbus began to hear whispers of mutiny.

Columbus discovers
the New World

1484

1493

Columbus plans his
grand Enterprise of
the Indies

1492

Columbus begins
his second voyage

In 1488, Portuguese mariner Bartolomeu Dias sailed south along the west coast of Africa and accidentally discovered the Cape of Good Hope. His discovery opened the way to an eastern sea route to India and the Far East.

He finally promised his men they would turn back if they did not sight land within three more days.

At about ten at night on October 11, 1492, a sailor named Rodrigo de Triana sighted a dim light ahead. It looked like the flickering light of a wax candle and soon disappeared. Columbus, as reported in his journal, assembled his crew and "urged them to keep a good look-out . . . and to watch carefully for land," promising "a silk doublet [a

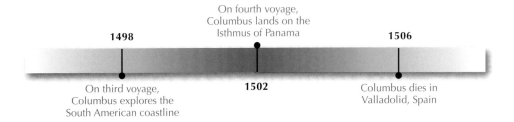

On fourth voyage, Columbus lands on the Isthmus of Panama

1498   1506

1502

On third voyage, Columbus explores the South American coastline

Columbus dies in Valladolid, Spain

Columbus searched for eight years for someone to fund his first voyage of discovery to the New World. Spanish monarchs Ferdinand V (left) and Isabella I (right) finally agreed to back his "Enterprise of the Indies."

close-fitting jacket worn by European men at the time] . . . to him who first sighted it."[1] A cry of land rang out within hours. "Two hours after midnight land appeared," Columbus noted, "at a distance of about two leagues [roughly six nautical miles]."[2]

After daybreak, Columbus put on a scarlet doublet and went ashore with a royal standard of Spain in hand. He knelt and kissed the shore of an unknown island and claimed it *"por Castilla y por León"*[3]—for Castile and for León. (Castile and León represented the separate Span-

1484

Columbus plans his
grand Enterprise of
the Indies

Columbus discovers
the New World

1492

1493

Columbus begins
his second voyage

ish kingdoms of Isabella and Ferdinand. Strictly speaking, Spain did not exist as a unified nation until 1516.) Natives called the island Guanahaní. Columbus renamed it San Salvador (for the "Savior"). The question then and now is, just what island was it?

Through the ages, experts have proposed no fewer than nine islands as the site of Columbus's historic landfall in the Bahamas. They comprise the present-day Cat, Conception, Plana Cays, Mayaguana, East Caicos, Grand Turk, Egg, Watlings, and Samana Cay. Geographers generally favored Watlings Island as the landing site during much of the twentieth century. They even renamed the island San Salvador. More recent studies prefer Samana Cay or Grand Turk over the others. Absolute proof still eludes the experts. Name changes to many of the islands further confuse the issue.

After his initial landfall, Columbus sailed on. He named a second island Santa Maria de la Concepción. Its name was later changed to Crooked Island and later still to Caicos. Atwood Island became Samana Cay. An island called Fernandina by Columbus eventually took on the name of Long Island or Mayaguana. Isabella changed to Fortune Island and then to Great and Little Inagua. Columbus concluded that these small islands must be offshore islands close to the Asian continent.

Continuing his search for Cipango, Columbus explored the northern coast of Cuba, which he mistook for the mainland of Cathay. His tiny fleet continued on to another large island, which Columbus named *La Española*. Known today as Hispaniola (his-pan-YOH-la), it is shared by the nations of Haiti and the Dominican Republic.

On Christmas Eve 1492, while exploring the coast of Hispaniola, the *Santa Maria* ran aground on a coral reef. Ever resourceful, Columbus salvaged timbers and planking from his flagship and constructed a

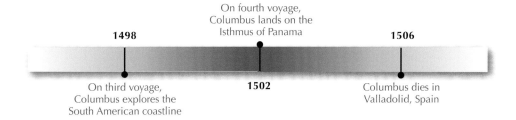

On fourth voyage, Columbus lands on the Isthmus of Panama

1498

1506

On third voyage, Columbus explores the South American coastline

1502

Columbus dies in Valladolid, Spain

trading post on the island. He named it, appropriately, *La Navidad* (Christmas) and left forty men there. On January 16, 1493, Columbus sailed for home with the *Niña* and the *Pinta*. He was already planning a second voyage to find the elusive Cipango.

In April 1493, Columbus appeared before Ferdinand and Isabella in Barcelona to report on his historic voyage. He spoke of the islands he had visited and of naked inhabitants, spices, plants, and medicinal trees. As proof of his findings, he displayed an odd assortment of samplings brought back from his voyage. They included parrots in cages, salted fish, skins of giant lizards, several Indians, and numerous precious gems and gold artifacts. Columbus concluded his royal visit with a kind

This replica of Columbus's flagship *Santa Maria* depicts the three-masted, square-rigged cargo vessel that carried him and his crew on their first voyage of discovery. The original *Santa Maria* ran aground on a coral reef near Hispaniola.

of fifteenth-century sales pitch for a second voyage: "I make this promise, that supported by only small aid from them I will give our invincible sovereigns as much gold as they need, as much spices, cotton . . . as much of the wood of the aloe, as many slaves to serve as

Columbus discovers
the New World

1484

1493

1492

Columbus plans his
grand Enterprise of
the Indies

Columbus begins
his second voyage

sailors as their Majesties wish to demand."[4] His dramatic presentation at court won him quick support for a second voyage. On September 25, 1493, Columbus sailed from Cádiz, Spain, with a fleet of seventeen ships and 1,200 to 1,500 men—sailors, soldiers, priests, and settlers.

On his second voyage (1493–1496), and on two subsequent voyages (1498–1500 and 1502–1504), Columbus expanded his exploration of what he believed to be the East Indies and the Asian mainland. Apart from the Gulf coasts of Mexico and the United States, his area of discovery eventually covered the entire Caribbean, including the West Indies and the Gulf coasts of Central and South America. Columbus died in Valladolid, Spain, in 1506, still believing he had found a westward sea route to the Orient.

The *Niña* and the *Pinta* (docked at the wall) sailed with the *Santa Maria*, the flagship of Christopher Columbus on his first voyage to the New World. The *Niña* and the *Pinta* were caravels—light trading vessels—that carried crews of eighteen men.

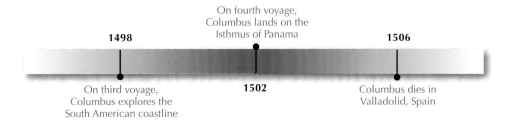

On fourth voyage, Columbus lands on the Isthmus of Panama

1498

1506

On third voyage, Columbus explores the South American coastline

1502

Columbus dies in Valladolid, Spain

Columbus's tomb in Seville Cathedral is one of several sites claiming to hold his remains. Tombs at the Columbus Lighthouse in the Dominican Republic and in Havana, Cuba, also claim to hold the remains of the great discoverer.

Even before Columbus's death, however, other explorers doubted that he had found a new route to the Far East. Some were already referring to his discoveries as part of the *Mundus Novus* (MOON-dus NO-vus), or New World. Despite his misguided geography, Columbus opened the door of the New World for European exploration and settlement—particularly the vast area that is now known as Latin America. The ensuing chapters will carry the reader back in time on a voyage of rediscovery in a sea of changing names and places. Ports of call will provide a glimpse of the origins and growth of the nations south of the United States in the Western Hemisphere.

The Voyages of Columbus

Christopher Columbus followed his historic voyage of 1492 with three lesser-known voyages to the New World. On his second voyage (1493–1496), he left Cádiz, Spain, on September 25, 1493, and made landfall on Dominica in the center of the Lesser Antilles on November 3. Sailing north along the chain of Leeward Islands, he explored and named Guadalupe (now Guadeloupe), San Martin (Nevis), and Santa Cruz (St. Croix). After exploring an island group he called the Virgin Islands, he sailed on to Hispaniola.

There, he found his trading post at La Navidad had been destroyed and its settlers killed by Carib Indians. Columbus chose to establish another settlement, Isabela, farther along on the island's north coast. He later abandoned it and set up a third colony on the island's south coast, calling it Santo Domingo. It has survived the ages as the capital of the Dominican Republic. Columbus spent several months exploring the south coast of Cuba. He sailed as far as the Isle of Pines (now *Isla de la Juventud*, or Isle of Youth) and discovered Jamaica before heading home in 1496.

Isla de la Juventud (Isle of Youth)

Columbus continued to explore what he thought was the East Indies on his third voyage in 1498. Sailing farther south than ever before, he circled around Trinidad and entered what is now the Gulf of Paria off the northeast coast of present-day Venezuela. He later sailed to Hispaniola and then home, arriving in Cádiz at the end of October 1500.

On his fourth voyage (1502–1504), Columbus concluded his explorations in the New World. This time, he landed at Martinique, sailed north past the Leeward Islands again, and west past Hispaniola. Turning south, he reached the northern coast of modern-day Honduras in early August 1503. Searching in vain for a passage through the land mass, he sailed south, passing the regions that now constitute Nicaragua and Costa Rica. From the Isthmus of Panama, he headed toward Jamaica, where he was stranded for over a year. He then stopped at Santo Domingo before returning home. He died not knowing his voyages had opened a New World for further exploration.

The Americas in the 1780s

Disputed by England, Russia, and Spain

Viceroyalty of New Spain

Effective Frontier of Spanish Settlement

Gulf of Mexico

Mexico City

Veracruz

Santo Domingo

Caribbean Sea

NORTH ATLANTIC OCEAN

Dutch Colonies

French Guyana

Viceroyalty of New Granada

Viceroyalty of Peru

Lima

PACIFIC OCEAN

Viceroyalty of Brazil

Rio de Janeiro

Viceroyalty of La Plata

Buenos Aires

SOUTH ATLANTIC OCEAN

Audiencia of Chile

N
W E
S

1000km

A viceroyalty was the largest administrative subdivision of the Spanish Empire in the Americas. Spain created four viceroyalties—New Spain, Peru, New Grenada, and La Plata. Portugal created a fifth viceroyalty in Brazil.

Chapter 2

New Spain: The Coming of the Conquistadors

Columbus opened the New World to Spain. Spanish conquistadors (conquerors) followed almost immediately. Conquistadors were adventurers who took part in Spain's conquest of the Americas in the sixteenth century. They were known both for their bravery and their brutality. They established colonies in the islands now known as the West Indies. Soon afterward, they spread Spain's influence to Central and South America.

In 1493, Diego Velásquez de Cuéllar sailed with Columbus to Hispaniola. He was one of the first conquistadors to arrive in the islands. Beginning in 1511, Velásquez conquered and colonized Cuba. He became its first governor in 1514.

In 1517, Velásquez sent Francisco Fernández de Córdoba to explore the mainland of what is now Mexico. A year later, he sent Juan de Grijalba on a similar expedition. Both men found gold and traces of advanced civilizations. Historians credit Grijalba with being the first to call the region "New Spain." Velásquez promptly sent Hernán Cortés to the mainland to check on reports of its gold and inhabitants.

On February 18, 1519, Cortés sailed with about 500 soldiers, 100 sailors, and 16 horses. Soon after landing in Mexico, he established a port settlement that he named Villa Rica de la Vera Cruz (Rich Village of the True Cross). Its name was later shortened to simply Veracruz. It soon became the chief port for shipping New World riches to Spain. In August, Cortés marched inland to attack the Aztec capital of

Tenochtitlán (tay-notch-teet-LAN). The Aztecs were an advanced warrior culture that ruled over what is now central and south Mexico.

On the way to Tenochtitlán, Cortés enlisted the aid of thousands of Indians who resented Aztec rule. He used their help and the shock power of guns and horses to great advantage. Cortés captured the Aztec ruler Montezuma II and forced the surrender of his capital in 1521. On the ruins of Tenochtitlán, Cortés built Mexico City.

Cortés became the main man in the conquest and colonization of today's Mexico. His dual mission was to seize land for Spain and to spread Christianity. Bernal Díaz del Castillo went along with Cortés and wrote about the conquest of Mexico. Díaz claimed that he came to the New World "to serve God and His Majesty, to give light to those who were in darkness, and to grow rich, as all men desire to do."[1]

In the service of God and king, Cortés razed Aztec cities and toppled their idols. Over the next five years, he conquered the remaining Aztec lands. He also brought present-day Honduras and much of El Salvador and Guatemala under Spanish control. Scholars now credit Cortés and diseases brought by the Europeans—chiefly smallpox— with the destruction of the Aztec population. To keep control over the vast territory Cortés had conquered and ruled, Spain established the Viceroyalty (VISE-roi-il-tee) of New Spain in 1535.

A viceroyalty was the largest administrative subdivision of the Spanish empire in the Americas. It was governed by an agent of the crown called a viceroy (which means "in place of the king"). New Spain was the first of four Spanish viceroyalties in the New World. Spain followed with the Viceroyalties of Peru in 1542, New Granada in 1717, and Río de la Plata in 1776. The latter three were located in western, northern, and southern South America, respectively.

| 1511 | Córdoba explores what is now Mexico | 1518 | Cortés founds Veracruz; he attacks the Aztecs | 1521 | Spain establishes the Viceroyalty of New Spain |

Velásquez conquers and colonizes Cuba | 1517 | Grijalba calls the region "New Spain" | 1519 | The Aztecs surrender to Cortés; he builds Mexico City | 1535

Hernán Cortés meets Aztec chieftain Montezuma II. Cortés landed in Mexico in February 1519 with about 500 soldiers, 100 sailors, and 16 horses. Soon after landing, he marched inland and conquered the Aztecs. He built Mexico City on the ruins of the Aztec capital, Tenochtitlán.

1540

Coronado searches for the Seven Cities of Cibola

1542

Spain founds the Viceroyalty of Peru

1544

Spain establishes the Kingdom of Guatemala

Spain founds the Viceroyalty of New Granada

1717

Spain creates the Viceroyalty of Rio de la Plata; Guatemala City is built

1776

New Spain covered part of the southwest United States and all of Mexico and Central America north of Panama. It also included much of the West Indies and the Philippines in the west Pacific Ocean. Today, seven nations make up Central America. They are Belize, Costa Rica, El Salvador, Guatemala, Honduras, Nicaragua, and Panama. Belize was originally known as British Honduras. It evolved from a settlement of English log cutters. Belize remained largely free of Spanish control.

The vast size of viceroyalties made governing hard. For better control, Spain split them into *audiencias* and provinces. A province was the basic administrative unit. It was ruled by a governor. Provinces, in turn, came under the rule of an audiencia, or court of law. The court represented a district within the viceroyalty. For example, the Kingdom of Guatemala was an audiencia. It was founded in 1544 and stretched across much of Central America. Its ruling court was seated in the capital city of Santiago de Guatemala. In 1773, an earthquake demolished the city. The capital was moved to the present site of Guatemala City in 1776.

As the conqueror and ruler of New Spain, Cortés accrued the equivalent of millions of dollars in today's U.S. currency. He earned claim to numerous estates and titles, but he eventually tired of government and returned to Spain in 1540. Cortés died of dysentery in 1547 at the age of sixty-two.

After Cortés's departure, New Spain's first viceroy sent an expedition to search for the Seven Cities of Cibola. The Seven Cities represented a legendary realm rumored to contain gold and other riches. Francisco Vásquez de Coronado led the expedition. Cibola eluded him. He found only Zuni Indian villages. The golden realm, he

1511

Velásquez conquers and colonizes Cuba

1517

Córdoba explores what is now Mexico

1518

Grijalba calls the region "New Spain"

1519

Cortés founds Veracruz; he attacks the Aztecs

1521

The Aztecs surrender to Cortés; he builds Mexico City

Spain establishes the Viceroyalty of New Spain

1535

In 1540, Francisco Vásquez de Coronado led an expedition in search of the Seven Cities of Cibola. Instead of a city rich in gold and precious stones, he found only the pueblos of the Zuni Indians in New Mexico and a tribe of seminomadic Indians in Kansas. But his expedition led to future Spanish colonies in the American Southwest.

said later, "had not been found, nor had the teeming cities, the gold or the precious stones."[2] But his searchings—which ranged as far as present-day Kansas—provided the basis for Spain's future colonies in the American Southwest. Spaniards dominated the region for the next two centuries.

1540

Spain founds the Viceroyalty of Peru

1544

Spain founds the Viceroyalty of New Granada

1776

Coronado searches for the Seven Cities of Cibola

1542

Spain establishes the Kingdom of Guatemala

1717

Spain creates the Viceroyalty of Rio de la Plata; Guatemala City is built

Chapter 2

Spain's colonial empire began collapsing in the late 1700s. Two events in Europe triggered its decline—the French Revolution that began in 1789 and the ensuing wars of Napoleon. France invaded Spain in 1808. In a war that lasted until 1814, its cost in men and money weakened Spain's control over its colonies. Seizing the chance to gain independence from Spain, the colonies revolted. Mexico won its independence in 1821. This ended the Viceroyalty of New Spain. Guatemala and other Central American states briefly joined the short-lived Mexican empire.

In 1823, Costa Rica, El Salvador, Guatemala, Honduras, and Nicaragua broke away from Mexico. They formed a political union called the United Provinces of Central America. This union held together until 1838 when its members began to separate. Each state became an independent republic by 1841. Throughout the rest of the century, Mexico and the Central American republics grappled with the countless difficulties that came with independence. Wealthy landowners powered their way to control in some countries; ambitious dictators seized power in others. Economies struggled, border disputes raged, and rebellion ruled—none more so than in Mexico.

Mexico lost part of its northern lands to the Republic of Texas in its war for independence in 1836. Further land disputes led to war with the United States in 1846. Mexico surrendered more lands in the western and southwestern U.S. and in northern Mexico. Under the Treaty of Guadalupe Hidalgo in 1848, Mexico ceded almost all of present-day New Mexico, Utah, Nevada, Arizona, California, Texas, and Colorado to the United States.

Liberal reforms plunged Mexico into civil war in 1858. Three years later, Mexico stopped payments on its mounting foreign debts. Spain,

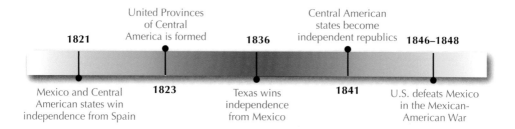

United Provinces of Central America is formed

1821

1836

Central American states become independent republics

1846–1848

Mexico and Central American states win independence from Spain

1823

Texas wins independence from Mexico

1841

U.S. defeats Mexico in the Mexican-American War

Great Britain, and France sent invasion forces to restore fiscal order. Spain and Great Britain soon withdrew their soldiers but French forces remained. On May 5, 1862, a Mexican army under General Ignacio Zaragoza defeated the French at Puebla. The victory is remembered today as the Cinco de Mayo—Fifth of May—celebration.

In 1864, Mexican conservatives overthrew the government of Benito Juárez. With the support of France, they installed Maximilian as emperor. Maximilian was the Archduke of Austria. He was meant to serve as an agent of French emperor Napoleon III, but he began acting on his own. After its own civil war ended in 1865, the United States intervened on behalf of Juárez. The Mexicans toppled Maximilian's regime and executed him in 1867. Disorder resumed in Mexico soon after Juárez died in office five years later.

Ferdinand Maximilian Joseph, Archduke of Austria and Emperor of Mexico, acted as an agent of the French occupation. When the French left Mexico, he was deposed and executed in 1867.

Mexico cried out for a strong leader. Porfirio Díaz, a decorated soldier, answered the call. He led a revolt and defeated government forces at the Battle of Tecoac in 1876. Díaz was formally elected

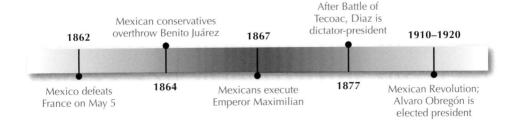

1862 — Mexico defeats France on May 5

Mexican conservatives overthrow Benito Juárez — 1864

1867 — Mexicans execute Emperor Maximilian

After Battle of Tecoac, Diaz is dictator-president — 1877

1910–1920 — Mexican Revolution; Alvaro Obregón is elected president

president in May 1877. He ruled from 1877 to 1880 and from 1884 to 1911 as Mexico's dictator-president. Díaz forged strong foreign investment policies. His vision greatly aided the development of Mexico's banking, agriculture, industry, mining, railroads, and telegraph system. But the people eventually tired of his tight control. The Mexican Revolution began in 1910 and forced him into exile in France the following year. Díaz died there in 1915. A succession of dictator-presidents followed Díaz. In 1920, the election of moderate President Alvaro Obregón marked the end of the Mexican Revolution and the beginning of a new era in Mexico.

Napoleon III, nephew of Napoleon Bonaparte and emperor of France. He installed Maximilian as emperor of Mexico. Maximilian's reign proved a disappointment to the French emperor.

The Mexican Revolution was the first great social revolt of the twentieth century. It was led by such rebels as Francisco "Pancho" Villa and Emiliano Zapata. Peasant-soldiers by the thousands responded to Zapata's call for "[r]eform, justice, freedom and law."[3] They marched for land and other reforms "glued to Zapata's horse's tail"[4]—that is, closely behind Zapata. More than a million people died in the long

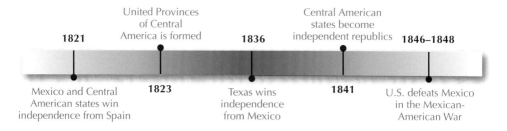

United Provinces of Central America is formed

1821

Central American states become independent republics

1836

1846–1848

Mexico and Central American states win independence from Spain

1823

Texas wins independence from Mexico

1841

U.S. defeats Mexico in the Mexican-American War

struggle. With some revisions, the constitution it fostered carried Mexico into the twenty-first century. Today, Mexico continues to seek solutions to social, economic, and political problems in a land of the very rich and the very poor.

Like Mexico, Central American countries struggled with stormy histories. They gained independence from Spain without violence in 1821. Thereafter, revolutions became common in the "banana republics." Costa Rica, El Salvador, Guatemala, Honduras, and Nicaragua all experienced multiple revolutions, civil wars, and boundary disputes. Along the way to the twenty-first century, all have fallen under

Francisco Villa (left) and Emiliano Zapata (second from right) played key roles in the Mexican Revolution (1910–1920). With Villa, Zapata occupied Mexico City and began to implement land reform. Both men died violently by the guns of opponents.

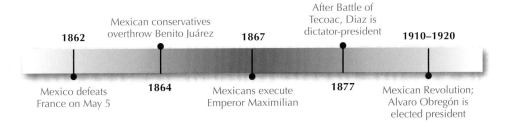

1862
Mexican conservatives overthrow Benito Juárez
1867
After Battle of Tecoac, Diaz is dictator-president
1910–1920

Mexico defeats France on May 5
1864
Mexicans execute Emperor Maximilian
1877
Mexican Revolution; Alvaro Obregón is elected president

Anastasio Somoza Garcia (center) with his sons Luis Somoza Debayle (left) and Anastasio Somoza Debayle. Like their father, both sons became powerful men in Nicaragua. Luis was president from 1956 to 1963. The younger Anastasio acted as dictator from 1963 until his assassination in 1979.

the sway of dictators and political dynasties. Notable among them were Manuel Estrada Cabrera of Guatemala and the Somoza family of Nicaragua. Cabrera ruled from 1898 to 1920; the Somozas reigned from 1937 to 1979.

Over the past five centuries, Mexico and the nations of Central America have defined their boundaries and carved out a place in the tropical sun. But even as New Spain gave way to Mexico and the modern nations of Central America, everything under the sun remains subject to change.

Banana Republics

The banana ranks as one of the world's most important food crops. Given its popularity among Americans, it might surprise many people to learn that it was unknown in the United States before 1870. And it was not until the 1880s that Americans discovered the commercial value of the banana. By the turn of the century, Americans were consuming more than sixteen million bunches a year.

Their passion for the fruit began in Costa Rica. In 1871, a young American named Minor Keith was building a railroad in that small Central American country. Keith recognized the potential U.S. market for bananas. He began planting bananas on either side of the railroad tracks. His plantings flourished. The completed railroad provided a cheap means of transporting the bananas for shipment to eager markets in the United States and elsewhere. In ten years, Keith owned three banana companies.

In 1899, Keith met with two other Americans, who owned the Boston Fruit Company. Their companies merged to form the United Fruit Company (UFCO), creating the largest banana company in the world. In addition to Costa Rica, UFCO owned plantations in Colombia, Cuba, Honduras, Jamaica, Nicaragua, Panama, the Dominican Republic, and Venezuela. Critics of UFCO credit it with turning these Latin American nations into "banana republics."

In his book *Cabbages and Kings*, American author O. Henry referred to Honduras as a "banana republic." The name soon became associated with all Latin American countries with banana-based economies. Political instability was common in many of these countries. Thus the name eventually came to mean

any dictator-ruled nation with a single-source economy, especially if the economy is controlled by foreign companies.

Companies like the United Fruit Company (left) did little to enhance the standard of living in their host countries. They supported corrupt regimes to their own benefit, and they took unfair advantage of cheap local labor. In 1970, UFCO merged with another company to become United Brands. The company encountered financial problems soon afterward and Del Monte Corporation acquired much of United Brands. Del Monte now operates most of United's former holdings with new emphasis on fair business practices. What was left of United Brands became Chiquita. Both companies continue to be active in the banana market.

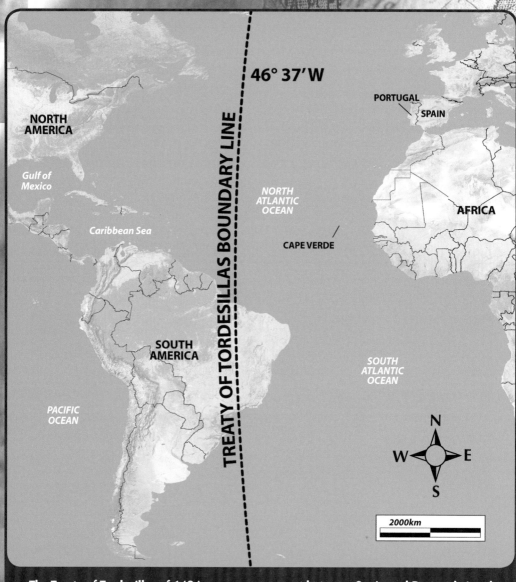

NORTH
AMERICA

Gulf of
Mexico

Caribbean Sea

SOUTH
AMERICA

PACIFIC
OCEAN

46° 37′W

TREATY OF TORDESILLAS BOUNDARY LINE

NORTH
ATLANTIC
OCEAN

CAPE VERDE

PORTUGAL

SPAIN

AFRICA

SOUTH
ATLANTIC
OCEAN

N
W   E
S

2000km

The Treaty of Tordesillas of 1494 was an agreement between Spain and Portugal aimed at settling disputes over territories discovered by explorers in the New World in the late fifteenth century. It established a line in the middle of the Atlantic Ocean. Spain claimed all new lands to the west of the line; Portugal, all new lands to the east of it.

Chapter 3

Kingdom of Brazil: Island of the True Cross

After Christopher Columbus discovered the New World, Spain claimed all rights to its conquest and settlement. Portugal immediately protested Spain's claim. The two Catholic countries called on Pope Alexander VI to settle their dispute. He drew an arbitrary line on a map from north to south in the middle of the Atlantic Ocean. The Treaty of Tordesillas (tor-day-SEEL-yas) of 1494 set that line at 370 leagues (1,177 nautical miles) west of the Cape Verde Islands. Spain received rights to all lands west of the line; Portugal got rights to those east of it.

On March 9, 1500, Portuguese nobleman Pedro Álvares Cabral led thirteen ships down the Tagus River from Lisbon and out to sea. He was bound for India to establish trading posts there. Cabral sailed first to the Cape Verde Islands, off the west coast of Africa. Then, in a maneuver called a *volta*, he veered westward to take advantage of the Atlantic winds and currents. By chance or design—no one knows for sure—Cabral kept sailing westward until he sighted land on April 22, 1500.

The land Cabral sighted was the now-famous Mount Pascal, which lies 500 miles north of modern-day Rio de Janeiro. Cabral sailed on to investigate. He landed at a little inlet he called Porto Seguro (meaning "safe port") and claimed the land for King Manuel I of Portugal. Thinking he had landed on an island, he named it *Ilha da Vera Cruz*—Island of the True (or Holy) Cross.

Cabral was a knight in the Order of Christ. His name for his discovery came from his knightly banner of a red cross on a white field. When he realized he had not landed on an island, he changed the name from *Ilha* to *Terra* (land). Later, when traders began cutting brazilwood for its red dye, they changed the name again to *Terra da Brazil*, and still again to simply Brazil.

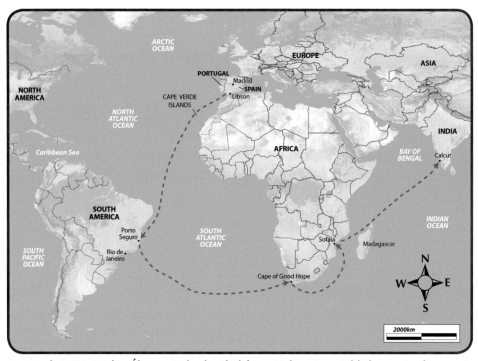

In March 1500, Pedro Álvares Cabral sailed from Lisbon to establish new trading ports in India. He veered westward to pick up favorable Atlantic winds and currents. Before correcting his course and completing his voyage to India, he sighted land that we now know as part of South America.

Cabral landed in what is now Brazil at a little inlet he called Porto Seguro ("safe port"). He explored the South American coastline for two weeks before sailing east for India.

Cabral explored the newly discovered coastline for two weeks and met a few local Indians. In a letter to Manuel I, he described them as "amiable and rustic."[1] He turned eastward in early May and successfully completed his voyage to India. After his return to Lisbon in 1501, Cabral retired to enjoy his wealth.

Initially, unlike Spain's colonies, Brazil did not offer the lure of rich gold and silver deposits. Accordingly, Portuguese settlers did not begin to arrive in Brazil until the 1530s. The *fidalgo* (fee-DAHL-go;

1638

The Portuguese found São Sebastião Rio de Janeiro

Portugal becomes a Spanish domain

1642

1647

Treaty of Madrid is signed

Brazilwood pods used to make red dye. Present-day Brazil owes its name to the trees bearing these pods.

nobleman) Martim Affonso de Souza founded the first Portuguese settlement on the island of São Vicente (near present-day Santos) in southern Brazil. Other settlements followed at Pernambuco (now Recife) and São Salvador (now Salvador or Bahia) in the northeast. King John III established captaincies—small hereditary kingdoms—in the coastal lands. He awarded captaincies to noblemen willing to develop them at their own expense. This allowed Portugal to ensure possession and control of the lands without cost to the Crown. Settlers in the northeast cultivated sugar cane plantations. Sugar exports flourished and eventually returned great wealth to Portugal. Cotton, tobacco, and cattle hides added further profits.

In the 1550s, a French expedition set up a colony in Guanabara Bay in southern Brazil. Their presence threatened to erode Portugal's profits and claims to the lands. After several attempts to dislodge the French, the Portuguese finally drove them out in 1567. On the site of the former French colony, the Portuguese raised a new city. They named it São Sebastião Rio de Janeiro for their reigning King Sebas-

1494

Pedro Álvares Cabral discovers Brazil

1530

French establish a colony at Guanabara Bay, Brazil

The Treaty of Tordesillas is signed

1500

Portuguese settlers arrive in Brazil

1550

tian. Reference to the king was later dropped from the city's name, which means "River of January."

Portuguese colonists relied on Indian slave labor to work on their plantations. Many Indians died from European diseases or fought the Portuguese and were killed. Jesuit missionaries tried to protect the Indians from slavery but imposed their own strict religious code on them. The Indians eventually died out or were absorbed into a racially mixed society. Portugal shipped thousands of Africans to Brazil to replace them as slave laborers.

In the 1600s, Jesuit Antônio Viera preached that "Brazil has its body in America but its soul in Angola."[2] He called on Africans to endure slavery with good heart and await their reward in heaven. Africans continued to endure their slavery until Brazil abolished it in 1888.

As a result of marriages and political accords, Spain and Portugal merged from 1580 to 1640. Portugal became a Spanish domain. Holland, as Portugal's former partner, lost business. In return, the Dutch invaded large areas of the Brazilian coast. They built forts, founded cities, and developed existing cities such as Recife. Portugal regained its freedom from Spain in 1640 and elevated Brazil to viceroyalty status with its capital at Salvador. The Portuguese immediately began a campaign to regain the territory the Dutch had taken. After fourteen years of war, they succeeded in driving the Dutch out of Brazil.

In the late 1600s and early 1700s, Portuguese settlers and fortune seekers moved westward. Paulists, who were adventurers from São Paulo, discovered gold and diamonds in what are now the Brazilian states of Minas Gerais and Mato Grosso. Thousands of Portuguese poured into these regions and pushed the limits of the Tordesillas line.

Portugal becomes a Spanish domain

1638

1647

1642

The Portuguese found São Sebastião Rio de Janeiro

Treaty of Madrid is signed

A terrance or pit mine in Minas Gerais. In the late 1600s and early 1700s, fortune seekers found gold and diamonds in what are now the Brazilian states of Minas Gerais and Mato Grosso.

Portugal and Spain signed the Treaty of Madrid in 1750. The treaty honored Portugal's claim to almost all of what makes up today's Brazil. Sugar and gold became Brazil's major exports, and Portugal grew richer.

In 1763, Portugal moved the capital from Salvador to Rio de Janeiro to accommodate the fast-growing southern region. By about 1800, some 100,000 people lived in the city, in a viceroyalty with a popula-

1815

Portugal declares
Brazil a kingdom

Emperor Pedro I
proclaims Brazil
independent

1822

1865–1870

Brazil, Argentina, and
Uruguay defeat Paraguay in
the War of the Triple Alliance

tion numbering more than 3.5 million colonists and slaves. In 1815, Portuguese King John VI declared Brazil a kingdom and appointed his son, Pedro I, its emperor in 1821. The new ruler proclaimed Brazil independent the following year. When Pedro lost territory that is now the nation of Uruguay in a war with Argentina, he deferred his rule to his five-year-old son, Pedro II. At age fifteen, Pedro II, said, "I am ready,"[3] and took the throne in 1841.

Pedro II presided over an era of great progress in Brazil. Railroads and telegraph lines opened new avenues of communication. A modern banking system lent support for developing commerce and industries, such as textiles, mining, agriculture, and ranching. New schools opened with a promise of improved futures for Brazilians. Coffee became a premium crop in the south. And increasing worldwide demand for rubber products led to the development of the Amazon region in the northwest.

Under Pedro, Brazil joined Argentina and Uruguay in defeating Paraguay in the War of the Triple Alliance (1865–1870). The war established Brazil's present boundary with Paraguay. When Pedro freed the slaves in 1888, however, he angered powerful slave owners. They backed a military coup that removed him from his throne and founded a republic in 1889. General Manoel Deodoro da Fonseca won election as Brazil's first president. Today, Brazilians honor Pedro II as a national hero.

Fonseca's election ushered in a period of large-scale European immigration and industrial growth, along with suspensions of civil rights and internal military coups that occurred off and on throughout much of the twentieth century. Externally, Brazil joined the Allies— chiefly, Great Britain, France, and the United States—in both World

1889

Brazilian republic
is founded

Brasilia becomes
capital of Brazil

1960

1985

Brazil returns to
civilian rule

Wars, and it became one of the original members of the United Nations in 1945.

In 1956, President Juscelino Kubitschek began to build a new capital named Brasilia on the Paraná River in the nation's interior. He described it as a town where everyone, regardless of social position, could benefit from "conditions of physical and moral safety appropriate for the harmonious development of human nature."[4] Brazil's seat

War of the Triple Alliance. In the War of the Triple Alliance (1865–1870), Argentina, Brazil, and Uruguay defeated Paraguay to firmly establish the borders of all four countries. Paraguay lost half of its population and much of its land.

1815

Portugal declares
Brazil a kingdom

Emperor Pedro I
proclaims Brazil
independent

1822

1865–1870

Brazil, Argentina, and
Uruguay defeat Paraguay in
the War of the Triple Alliance

From Portugal's earliest colonies in Brazil in the 1530s, and despite the limitations of the Tordesillas line, Brazil has emerged as the largest nation on the developing South American continent. It is also the continent's most populous country and boasts of a growing economy.

1889 — Brazilian republic is founded

Brasilia becomes capital of Brazil

1960

1985 — Brazil returns to civilian rule

of government moved from Rio de Janeiro to Brasilia in 1960. Construction of the new capital aided the development of the nation's interior but heightened its inflation rate. So far, the dream of Brasilia remains unfulfilled.

After almost a century of mostly military-controlled governments, Brazil returned to civilian rule in 1985. Brazil closed out the twentieth century in the throes of a deep depression, and scandals in high places continued to taint its left-leaning government. Even so, the economy of South America's largest and most populous country was growing, and its trade surplus was setting a record high early in the twenty-first century. In the land of joyous dances such as the samba and the bossa nova, Brazilians can still find cause to celebrate Carnival and face the future with optimism.

President Juscelino Kubitschek built a new capital named Brasilia on the Paraná River in the nation's interior. Brazil's seat of government moved from Rio de Janeiro to Brasilia in 1960.

Carnival

Modern Brazil is famous for its coffee, its soccer teams, and its Amazonian rain forests. But perhaps nothing better symbolizes the world's fifth most populous nation than its Carnival (or *Carnaval* in Portuguese). The Brazilian Carnival (below) is an annual event similar to Mardi Gras in New Orleans. It begins forty days before Easter and marks the start of Lent, a period of Christian fasting which imitates Jesus' fasting in the wilderness.

In practice, Carnival affords fun-loving Brazilians—and partyers from around the world—a final fling of four days of music and dancing, food, spirits, and forbidden pleasures before fasting. "Fasting" during Lent generally involves not eating certain foods rather than not eating at all. The name Carnival itself derives from *carnevale*, Latin for "removal of meat" (and thus abstaining from certain foods when fasting). Brazilians celebrate the annual holiday across the country, but particularly in Salvador da Bahia and Rio de Janeiro, both former capitals.

Carnival began in Rio de Janeiro in the 1830s. The city's middle-class citizens borrowed the practice of holding balls and masquerade parties from Paris. Parisians found their inspiration for the celebration much farther back in time. Carnival originated as an ancient Greek spring fertility rite honoring Dionysus, the god of wine.

In Rio, Carnival features extravagant parades put on by the city's major samba schools in the huge Sambódromo Stadium. Tens of thousands of dancers, singers, and drummers surround scores of spectacular floats and parade in elaborate costumes—or in no costumes at all—in an epic event televised around the world. Elsewhere in the city, groups of costumed people called blocos (blocks) revel and dance wildly through the streets to the primitive beat of drums and the infectious rhythms of the samba.

In Salvador, the former home of the Portuguese sugar industry and slave trade, Carnival emphasizes African music, and celebrants roam cobblestone streets amid colonial architecture to the unique beat of Bahian drummers. Bahian entertainer Carlinhos Brown explains, "We play, not for money, but to celebrate our happiness. Our carnival . . . is for everyone, not just for those with money."[5] At Carnival time in Brazil, even the poorest of the poor rejoice.

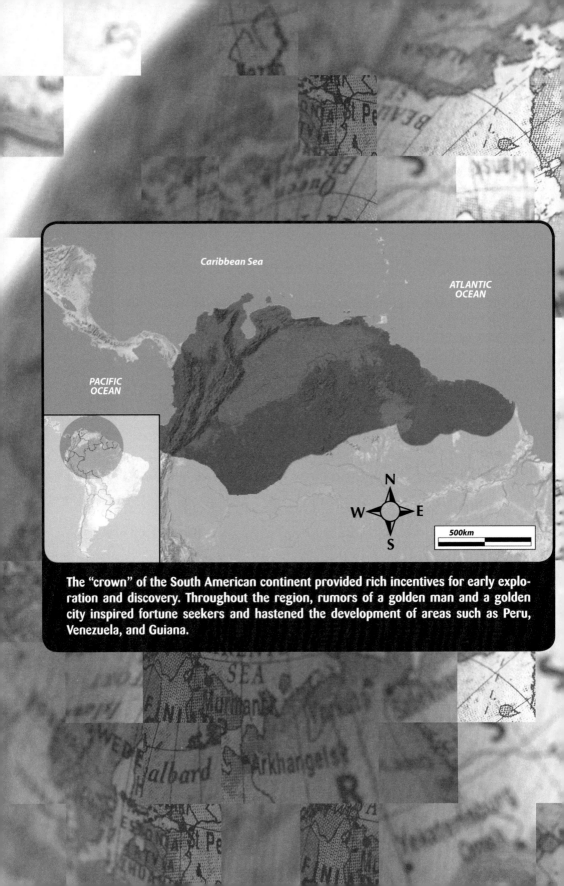

Caribbean Sea

ATLANTIC
OCEAN

PACIFIC
OCEAN

N
W ✦ E
S

500km

The "crown" of the South American continent provided rich incentives for early exploration and discovery. Throughout the region, rumors of a golden man and a golden
city inspired fortune seekers and hastened the development of areas such as Peru,
Venezuela, and Guiana.

Chapter 4

Guiana: The Search for El Dorado

Due north of Brazil, on the north-central coast of South America, lies the region known as Guiana. Its boundaries are roughly defined by the Orinoco, Negro, and Amazon Rivers and the Atlantic Ocean. Christopher Columbus explored its coastline during his third voyage to the New World in 1498. The next year, Italian navigator Amerigo Vespucci further explored the South American coast for Spain. He traced its shoreline from Cape São Roque in Brazil to the mouth of the Orinoco in present-day Venezuela. Spanish explorer Vicente Pinzón visited the Guiana coast in 1500. Spain claimed the region between the Amazon and Orinoco deltas in 1593 but made no attempt to settle it because of its dense terrain and hostile environment.

Long before this claim, far to the west, rumors had begun to build about a golden (or gilded) man called El Dorado (ell-duh-RAH-doh). Amerindians (a-meh-RIN-dee-ans; American Indians) told Spanish conquistadors about a curious rite that took place at an inland lake called Guatavita, near what is now Bogotá, Colombia. The rite centered on the initiation of a new ruling prince. As legend had it, the new ruler, with his main chieftains and great piles of gold and emeralds, was floated out on the water on a raft of rushes. According to Juan Rodríquez Freyle, writing in 1636, the prince was then "stripped to his skin, and anointed with a sticky earth on which they placed gold dust so that he was completely covered with this metal . . . when they reached the centre of the lagoon . . . the gilded Indian made his offering, throwing out all the pile of gold into the middle of the lake,

Statue of Amerigo Vespucci, the Italian navigator who explored the South American coast for Spain. The terms *America* and *New World* were first used to describe the places he visited.

and the chiefs who accompanied him did the same."[1]

At first, this legend inspired fortune hunters to seek gold and emeralds unsuccessfully at the bottom of Lake Guatavita. In time, *El Dorado* came to mean both a golden man and a mythical golden city known to Amerindians as Manoa. As the legend spread, so did the search for El Dorado.

Following the lure of the "golden man," captains of conquistador Francisco Pizarro searched to the south and east of Bogotá. Diego de Almagro found no gold but led the first European exploration of present-day Chile in 1535. In 1542, Francisco de Orellana failed to find El Dorado. Instead, he became the first European to successfully navigate the length of the Amazon River. He traced it from its source in the foothills of the Peruvian Andes to its mouth at what is now Belém, Brazil.

Orellana named the river after a dozen warrior women he met along the way. Friar Gaspar de Carvajal, the expedition's official chron-

1498
Christopher Columbus explores South American coastline

Diego de Almagro explores Chile
1535

1542
Francisco de Orellana navigates the Amazon River

Spain claims the Guiana region
1593

Present-day Kaiapo Amerindians. *Amerindian* is a term applied to a member of any of the native peoples of the Western Hemisphere, except for the Eskimos and the Aleuts.

icler, described them as "very robust" and "doing as much fighting as ten men."[2] The name reflects their similarity to the Amazons of Greek legend, a tribe of warrior women who lived north of the Black Sea.

Perhaps the most famous seeker of the golden myth was Sir Walter Raleigh. The English adventurer and man-about-court hoped to find Manoa deep in the forests beyond the Orinoco River, in present-day Venezuela. He sailed for Guiana in 1595. His first expedition failed at the mouth of the Caroní River when the rains came and the swollen river posed an impossible barrier. He later wrote, "[T]he river began to rage and overflow very fearfully, and the rains came down in terrible showers and gusts, in great abundance, and withal [with that] our men

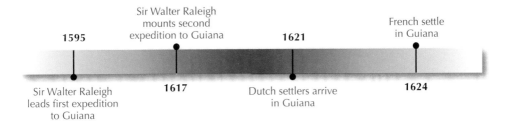

1595

Sir Walter Raleigh
leads first expedition
to Guiana

Sir Walter Raleigh
mounts second
expedition to Guiana

1617

1621

Dutch settlers arrive
in Guiana

French settle
in Guiana

1624

began to cry out for want of shift."[3] Raleigh turned around and returned to England, disappointed but only temporarily discouraged.

In 1617, Raleigh sailed again for Guiana. He fell ill at Trinidad and remained there, but his expedition again proceeded up the Orinoco. In a tussle with Spaniards at San Thomé—now Ciudad Guayana or San Tomé de Guayana—Raleigh's son Wat was killed. That brought an end

The rumor of El Dorado—the golden or gilded man—probably originated with the initiation rites of an Amerindian prince as a new chieftain. The ceremony took place at Lake Guatavita, near present-day Bogotá. The prince was covered with gold dust and floated out on the sacred lake to offer treasures to the Guatavita goddess. This model of the ceremony is in the Gold Museum in Bogotá.

Diego de Almagro
explores Chile

Spain claims the
Guiana region

1498   1542

Christopher Columbus   1535   Francisco de   1593
explores South   Orellana navigates
American coastline   the Amazon River

to the expedition. Raleigh returned to England, this time to face disgrace and execution. El Dorado remained somewhere beyond the next river or just over the next hill. In truth, it existed—and yet exists—only in the mind's eye.

If nothing else, the legend of El Dorado opened up Guiana and other difficult South American regions to exploration. It provided impetus not only to the Spaniards in Venezuela and elsewhere, but also to the English, Dutch, and French in Guiana. Despite Spain's claim to the region, the Dutch began to settle along the Essequibo, Courantyne, and Cayenne Rivers in 1602. The Dutch West India Company arrived in 1621. In mid-century, the trading company brought in African slaves to work its coffee, cotton, and tobacco plantations.

Sir Walter Raleigh with his son Wat. Raleigh traveled to Guiana twice in search of El Dorado. Wat was killed on his second trip.

In 1651, English planters in Barbados saw opportunities arising in Guiana and sent settlers and their slaves to Dutch Guiana. Holland resented England's intrusion in its colony. To protect Holland's interests, a Dutch fleet seized Dutch Guiana in 1667. That same year, the

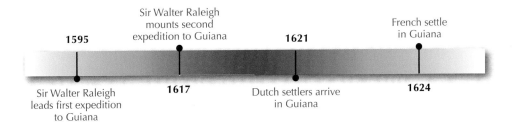

Sir Walter Raleigh mounts second expedition to Guiana

1595

French settle in Guiana

1621

Sir Walter Raleigh leads first expedition to Guiana

1617

Dutch settlers arrive in Guiana

1624

Devil's Island lies off the north coast of French Guiana. In 1852, French Emperor Napoleon III authorized its use as a penal colony. France abolished its penal colonies in 1938. The last prisoner left Devil's Island in 1953.

Treaty of Breda resolved their difficulties. It awarded Dutch Guiana to the Dutch and Nieuw Amsterdam (New York) to the English in exchange.

Meanwhile, the French were not to be denied a presence in South America. In 1624, they set up a trading post at Sinnamary to the east of Dutch Guiana and founded the town of Cayenne in 1643. In addition to settling British-Dutch differences, the Treaty of Breda also awarded the region now known as French Guiana to France.

Sugar became the chief crop in the Dutch-ruled coastal region of Guiana in the 1700s. A wave of British planters streamed into the area between 1742 and 1786. The new influx greatly increased the use of

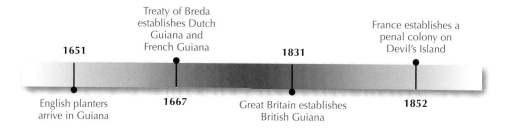

Treaty of Breda establishes Dutch Guiana and French Guiana

1651

1831

France establishes a penal colony on Devil's Island

English planters arrive in Guiana

1667

Great Britain establishes British Guiana

1852

slaves. During the French Revolution (1789–99) and Napoleon's ensuing conquest of Europe, the British temporarily occupied the Dutch-held Guiana territories. Further British-Dutch differences were settled after Napoleon's defeat in 1815, when Great Britain bought the Dutch colonies at Denerara, Berbice, and Essequibo.

In 1831, Britain consolidated its holdings into British Guiana. The new British colony abolished slavery in 1834. French Guiana and Dutch Guiana followed suit in 1848 and 1863, respectively. Most of the freed slaves refused to return to the plantations. As a result, planters brought in replacements from India, China, and Southeast Asia, resulting in a highly mixed racial makeup in the region.

In 1852, France brought attention to the region when it established a penal colony on the notorious Devil's Island, off the north coast of French Guiana. British settlers drew even greater attention to the area with the discovery of gold in 1879. Their discovery initiated a rush to exploit the region's mineral resources. After the discovery of bauxite, the chief source of aluminum, in 1917, mining became the principal industry of British and Dutch Guiana.

In 1946, French Guiana became a French overseas *département* (department), a designation given to French

Bauxite, the chief source of aluminum, was discovered in the Guiana region in 1917. After its discovery, mining became the principal industry of British and Dutch Guiana.

1946

British Guiana becomes
independent Guyana

1975

French Guiana becomes a
French overseas department

1966

Dutch Guiana becomes
independent Suriname

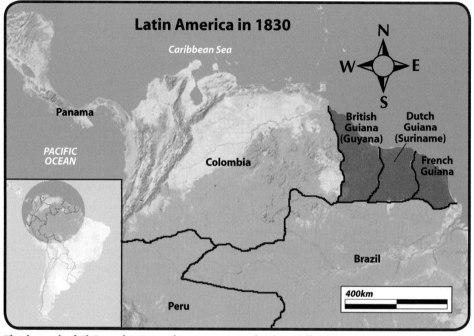

The legend of El Dorado opened up Guiana and other difficult South American regions to exploration. English, Dutch, and French settlers streamed into Guiana seeking their fortunes. The three Guianas evolved into the present-day nations of Guyana, Suriname, and French Guiana.

colonies. In 1964, Britain introduced a new system of government in British Guiana. A representative government led to its independence as the new nation of Guyana in 1966. Lastly, Dutch Guiana achieved independence as Suriname in 1975. Along with Brazil, the three nations founded in Guiana represent the only non-Spanish speaking countries of Latin America.

Devil's Island

Seeing Devil's Island (or *Île de Diable* in French) from afar, an observer might mistake the rocky, palm-covered isle for a vision of tropical paradise. On closer examination, a very different image emerges. It ranks high—if not highest—among history's most infamous prisons.

Devil's Island lies about ten miles off the mainland of French Guiana, at the mouth of the Kourou River. Along with Royale and St. Joseph Islands, it forms the *Îles du Salut* (Safety Islands). The name originated with a group of colonists who fled to the islands in the 1760s to escape the unhealthy lowlands around Kourou on the mainland. Kourou is now the site of the French space center. Devil's Island, measuring only 3,900 feet (1,200 meters) long and 1,320 feet (400 meters) wide, is the smallest of the three islets.

In 1852, French Emperor Napoleon III authorized its use as a penal colony. The prison actually consisted of the island group and additional facilities on the mainland at Kourou. The entire penal settlement was known collectively as Devil's Island and was maintained separately from the department of French Guiana. The French called it *bagne de Cayenne* (prison of Cayenne) after the capital of French Guiana.

Prison block on Devil's Island

Actually, very few prisoners were confined on Devil's Island itself. Most served their sentences on the mainland. Prisoners sentenced to less than an eight-year term had to serve an equal time on the mainland to earn passage back to Europe; those serving terms of more than eight years had to remain in French Guiana permanently. Beginning in 1885, only criminals sentenced to more than eight years were sent to Devil's Island.

Few prisoners managed to escape Devil's Island. The steamy, disease-ridden penal colony offered only three routes to freedom: by sea, across neighboring Dutch Guiana, or overland to Brazil. Escape by sea required a seaworthy craft and navigational skills; by land, would-be escapees had to survive hundreds of miles of swamps and jungles. To more than 80,000 prisoners, Devil's Island amply demonstrated its reputation as a place of no return. France decided to abolish the Devil's Island penal colony in 1938. The last prisoner left in 1953.

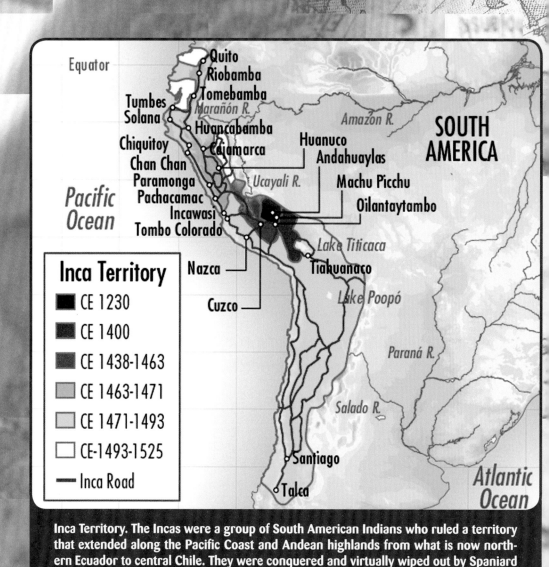

Equator

Quito
Riobamba
Tomebamba
Tumbes
Solana
Marañón R.
Huancabamba
Chiquitoy
Cajamarca
Chan Chan
Paramonga
Pachacamac
Incawasi
Tombo Colorado

Amazon R.

**SOUTH
AMERICA**

Huanuco
Andahuaylas
Ucayali R.
Machu Picchu
Oilantaytambo

**Pacific
Ocean**

Nazca

Cuzco

Tiahuanaco

Lake Titicaca

Lake Poopó

Paraná R.

Salado R.

Inca Territory

- CE 1230
- CE 1400
- CE 1438-1463
- CE 1463-1471
- CE 1471-1493
- CE-1493-1525
- Inca Road

Santiago

Talca

**Atlantic
Ocean**

Inca Territory. The Incas were a group of South American Indians who ruled a territory that extended along the Pacific Coast and Andean highlands from what is now northern Ecuador to central Chile. They were conquered and virtually wiped out by Spaniard Francisco Pizarro.

Chapter 5

Inca Gold: Viceroyalty of Peru

West of Guiana and throughout the Western Hemisphere, nothing contributed more to the exploration and development of Latin America than the lure of gold. In 1502, Columbus made landfall on the Isthmus of Panama during his continuing search for Cipango and the East Indies. Eight years later, Spanish explorer Vasco Núñez de Balboa founded the first successful colony on the isthmus at Santa María la Antigua del Darién (now simply Darién).

At some point after the founding of Darién in 1510, Balboa began to hear stories from many Indians about the "Great Waters" beyond the mountains. One Indian boy spoke of a land of great wealth called Birú (Peru) that lay to the south. He told him, "If that is what you are willing to risk your lives for, I can tell you of a kingdom where they eat and drink from golden vessels and where gold is as plentiful as iron is with you."[1]

In 1513, Balboa followed the promise of gold through the dense Panamanian jungle to the great ocean beyond. Since it lay south of his vantage point, he named it the Mar del Sur (South Sea). With drawn sword and the banner of Castile and León, he waded into the water and claimed the ocean and all lands that it touched for Spain. Balboa little realized the enormity of his claim, for the sea was the greatest of them all—the Pacific Ocean. Balboa returned to Darién to find that Spain had sent Pedro Arias de Ávila (known as Pedrarias) to govern the region. Pedrarias became jealous of Balboa's growing prestige and influence in the area. He had Balboa seized, charged with treason,

53

Balboa takes possession of seas, lands, and coasts of the islands of the south in the name of Ferdinand and Isabella.

falsely convicted, and beheaded, abruptly ending Balboa's quest for riches.

One of the men in Balboa's party was a coarse soldier named Francisco Pizarro. As the illegitimate, illiterate son of a soldier, Pizarro saw no future for himself in Spain and migrated to the New World to seek his fortune. After serving with Balboa, he settled in the city of Panama (now Panama City) at age forty-two. The aging soldier soon felt drawn to the same rumors of a rich Indian empire to the south in Birú that had motivated Balboa. Inspired by the success of Hernán Cortés in New Spain, he took on Diego de Almagro as a business partner. Almagro was a soldier of similar background. Between 1524 and 1528, the pair made two voyages down the west coast of South America, sailing as far south as northern Chile.

Pizarro returned from the second voyage with a small amount of gold and news of an advanced Indian civilization—the Inca Empire. He sailed to Spain and presented his findings to the Spanish court

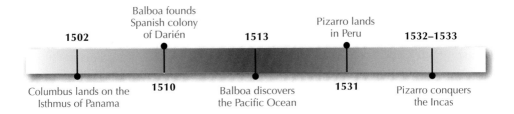

Balboa founds Spanish colony of Darién — 1513 · Pizarro lands in Peru · 1532–1533

1502 · Columbus lands on the Isthmus of Panama · 1510 · Balboa discovers the Pacific Ocean · 1531 · Pizarro conquers the Incas

PANAMA

Caribbean Sea

Panama City

ATLANTIC OCEAN

San Mateo Bay

Tumbes

Cajamarca

SOUTH AMERICA

N
W — E
S

Lima ◎ Cuzco

PACIFIC OCEAN

750km

Key

━━━━━ Pizarro's routes, 1524–1533

Between 1524 and 1533, Spanish conquistador Francisco Pizarro made three voyages to northwest South America. On his third voyage, he traveled overland to capture Cuzco, conquer the Incas, and found the city that is now Lima, Peru. This map represents a composite of Pizarro's travels.

Spain establishes the
Viceroyalty of Peru

1535

Peru defines its
present boundaries

1824

Pizarro founds his
capital at Lima, Peru

1542

Peru gains its
independence from Spain

1942

55

gathered at Toledo in 1529. King Charles I authorized him to explore and conquer the vast area. The king named him captain-general of the future Peru. Pizarro returned to Panama to prepare for his third and most important voyage. In late December 1530, he set sail with three ships and 180 men.

Pizarro arrived in Tumbes, an outlying coastal town of the Inca Empire in northwest Peru, the following spring. He had visited Tumbes on his second voyage. This time he found the town in ruins in the aftermath of a civil war between two Inca rulers, the brothers Atahualpa (at-uh-WALL-puh) and Huascar (WAHSS-kar). Atahualpa ruled in the north with headquarters in Quito (in modern Ecuador); his brother reigned in the south, based in Cuzco (now in Peru). In May 1532, with the Incas already divided, Pizarro set out to conquer them with 62 horsemen and 106 foot soldiers—and a talent for treachery. In the manner of Cortés in Mexico, he would rely on disciplined soldiers and the shock value of guns, armor, and horses to overcome much larger native forces.

Pizarro learned that Atahualpa was camped in the hills near the city of Cajamarca to the southeast. He headed that way, learning en route that Atahualpa had taken Huascar prisoner. In a show of friendship, Atahualpa sent an envoy bearing gold bracelets and other gifts to meet Pizarro's forces. Pizarro invited the Inca chieftain to meet him in Cajamarca for supposedly friendly talks. Atahualpa accepted his offer, and Pizarro took him captive, trapping him with concealed soldiers. Pizarro and his men then opened fire with cannons and muskets on thousands of Incas gathered in the town square. At least 2,000 and as many as 10,000 Incas died that day.

Balboa founds
Spanish colony
of Darién

1502   1513   Pizarro lands in Peru   1532–1533

Columbus lands on the   1510   Balboa discovers   1531   Pizarro conquers
Isthmus of Panama   the Pacific Ocean   the Incas

Capture of Atahualpa. Francisco Pizarro invited the Inca chieftain to meet him in Cajamarca for supposedly friendly talks. Atahualpa accepted his offer, and Pizarro took him captive. Pizarro and his conquistadors executed Atahualpa in July 1533.

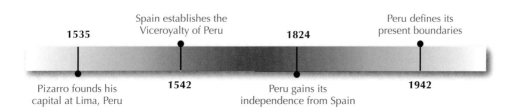

Spain establishes the Viceroyalty of Peru

Peru defines its present boundaries

1535

1824

Pizarro founds his capital at Lima, Peru

1542

Peru gains its independence from Spain

1942

Pizarro then realized that Atahualpa might bring a handsome ransom from his Inca subjects. He was right. For his release, the Incas offered and delivered a ransom of gold and silver large enough to fill a room. With ransom in hand, Pizarro charged Atahualpa with being "guilty of idolatry and adulterous practices, indulging openly in plurality of wives."[2] Atahualpa was tried, convicted, and executed in July 1533.

At about the same time, news reached Pizarro that Huascar had been killed by his guards. In the resulting chaos, Pizarro marched on Cuzco, taking the Royal Inca Highway through the other-

Francisco Pizarro founded the city of Lima on the Rimac River in 1535. The name derives from a corruption of the word *Rimac*.

wise impassable Andes range. He fought and won four battles along the way—at Jauja, Vilcashuaman, Vilaconga, and the pass overlooking Cuzco. When Pizarro arrived at Cuzco in November, he met no resistance. The Incas were defeated.

In January 1535, Pizarro founded his capital city on the Rimac River. He named it the "City of the Kings" (for the three kings in the

Balboa founds
Spanish colony
of Darién
1513

Pizarro lands
in Peru
1532–1533

1502

Columbus lands on the
Isthmus of Panama

1510

Balboa discovers
the Pacific Ocean

1531

Pizarro conquers
the Incas

Cuzco was founded around the eleventh century by Manco Capac. It was known as the "City of the Sun." Inca ruler Huascar made it his capital until Spanish conquistador Francisco Pizzaro defeated the Incas in 1533.

New Testament account of the birth of Jesus). It was later renamed Lima, through a corruption of the word *Rimac*. Within a year, a quarrel with Diego de Almagro erupted into a civil war. Pizarro quickly crushed his old partner and ordered his beheading. To deter further breaches of loyalties, he sent his conquistadors on exploratory expeditions into bordering regions. They included present-day Ecuador,

1535

Spain establishes the Viceroyalty of Peru

1824

Peru defines its present boundaries

Pizarro founds his capital at Lima, Peru

1542

Peru gains its independence from Spain

1942

Diego de Almagro quarreled with Francisco Pizarro and started a war. Pizarro quickly crushed his old partner and ordered his beheading.

Colombia, and Chile. Pizarro himself, now a rich man, had little time to enjoy his wealth. Almagro's illegitimate son murdered him in Lima on July 26, 1541—a brutal end to the life of a brutal conqueror.

In 1542, Spain established the Viceroyalty of Peru. Until the eighteenth century, it included all of Spanish South America except Venezuela.

Early in the nineteenth century, Latin Americans began to challenge the divine right of kings to rule, and the great independence movement commenced. Peru, first led by the Argentine soldier José Francisco de San Martín (see Chapter 8), and later by Simón Bolívar, declared its freedom in 1821 and achieved total independence from Spain in 1824. Disputes with Spain and neighbors Colombia, Ecuador, and Chile (in the War of the Pacific) continued into the twentieth century until Peru defined its present boundaries in 1942.

War of the Pacific

A world demand for nitrate provoked the War of the Pacific between Chile and the allied forces of Bolivia and Peru from 1879 to 1884. Nitrate is valuable for use as fertilizer and is a key element in explosives. High-quality deposits of nitrate—saltpeter and guano—were found in the Atacama Desert in the 1840s. The desert encompasses a desolate, 600-mile-long strip of land on the Pacific Coast of South America. The strip included the Peruvian regions of Tacna, Arica, and Tarapacá, and the Bolivian region of Antofagasta. These regions grew in strategic importance with the increasing world demand for nitrate. Conflicting claims over mining concessions led inevitably to war.

Peru seized property of Chilean nitrate companies in 1875. Bolivia did likewise in 1878. Chile immediately answered by voiding a border agreement with Bolivia and occupying the port of Antofagasta with 200 troops in February 1879. Bolivia declared war against Chile on March 1. Peru, honoring a secret alliance with Bolivia, joined the fight. On April 5, Chile declared war on both of the allies.

The first phase of the war was fought largely at sea. Chile's more powerful navy prevailed over the smaller Peruvian fleet in about six months. The war almost immediately moved on shore for its second phase. Chilean forces routed Peruvian-Bolivian armies in the Tarapacá region in late 1879. After occupying Antofagasta and Tarapacá, Chilean troops pressed northward and seized the towns of

Battle of Arica

Arica and Tacna in June 1880. In November, a Chilean force of some 25,000 men landed at Pisco, Peru, advanced north, and captured the Peruvian capital of Lima on January 16, 1881. The conflict turned into a war of attrition in which the forces of Chile gradually wore down those of Peru and Bolivia over the next two years.

In separate peace treaties—with Peru in 1883 and Bolivia in 1884—Chile gained possession of the Tarapacá region from Peru and the Antofagasta region from Bolivia. As a result, Bolivia lost its outlet to the sea. Bolivia averted a potentially devastating effect on its economy, however. Under the terms of the peace treaty, Chile guaranteed Bolivia freedom of transit for its commerce through Chilean lands and ports.

Santa Marta   Cumaná

**Viceroyalty
of New Granada**   **Guianas**

Sante Fe
de Bogatá

Audiencia of Peru

Amazon River

**Kingdom of
Brazil**

Lima

La Paz

**Audiencia
of
Upper Peru**

PACIFIC
OCEAN

Rio de Janeiro

SOUTH
ATLANTIC
OCEAN

Asunción

Tucumán

**Viceroyalty
of La Plata**

Montevideo

Santiago de Chile

Buenos Aires

N
W   E
S

750km

The Viceroyalty of New Granada crowned the South American continent.
Spain established New Grenada as a viceroyalty in 1717. It originally contained present-day Panama, Colombia, Venezuela, and Ecuador.

Chapter 6

Gran Colombia: Simón Bolívar and the Revolt against Spain

To the east and north of Peru lies the crown of South America and the linking finger of Central America. Eventually, the modern nations of Ecuador, Colombia, Panama, and Venezuela would emerge from this broad swath of land. Scholars have described this torrid region as the cradle of South America's independence from Spain.

Columbus first sighted the north coast of present-day Venezuela in 1498. The next year, Spanish navigator Alonso de Ojeda traced its coastline from the mouth of the Orinoco River to the Gulf of Venezuela. Because local fishermen built their houses over the water on stilts, he named the entire region Venezuela ("Little Venice"). Two decades later, Spanish missionary Bartolomé de Las Casas founded the first European settlement in South America at Cumaná. Cumaná lies some 185 miles (300 kilometers) east of Venezuela's capital of Caracas. It still exists as an important port city.

A few years later, in Santa Marta, a settlement on the Caribbean coast of present-day Colombia, the provincial governor wanted the terrain features of his province explored. He chose Gonzalo Jiménez de Quesada, a local official, for the mission. Part of Quesada's task was to try to reach Peru via the Magdalena River. He left Santa Marta in April 1536 with about 600 men. For months on end, Quesada and his men followed the rain-swollen banks of the river and hacked their way through snake-infested forests and swamps. By the time they reached the Colombian uplands in March 1537, only 166 men remained. After subduing the Tunja and Cundinamarca Indians, they

Gonzalo Jiménez de Quesada explored the Colombian highlands and named the region New Granada. Charles I of Spain named him marshal of New Granada.

reached the plateau of Bogotá, the home of the Chibcha Indians.

Quesada did not know it, but he had found the closest thing to El Dorado that anyone would ever find. The Chibchas were friendly and showered the Spaniards with gifts. Every man received gold hearts, each weighing two pounds. Quesada named the vast region he had conquered New Granada and founded the city of Santa Fe de Bogotá (now Bogotá). Charles I later named Quesada marshal of New Granada. The area now makes up Colombia, Panama, Venezuela, and Ecuador. New Granada came under the nominal control of the viceroy of Peru until becoming a separate viceroyalty in 1717.

As Spaniards settled in to the coastal plains—or *llanos* (LA-nos) in Spanish—they interbred with Carib Indians and later with slaves imported from Africa. These unions produced a mixed breed called *llaneros* (la-NAIR-ohs), or plainsmen. They became excellent horsemen and raised cattle. The export of hides formed a central part of the region's sluggish economy, but its exports

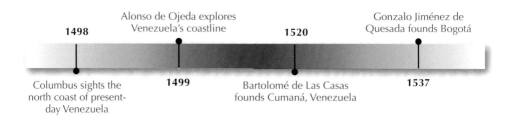

Alonso de Ojeda explores Venezuela's coastline

1498

Gonzalo Jiménez de Quesada founds Bogotá

1520

Columbus sights the north coast of present-day Venezuela

1499

Bartolomé de Las Casas founds Cumaná, Venezuela

1537

were insufficient to sustain a growing population. By the 1700s, Venezuela had become one of Spain's poorest South American colonies.

In 1718, to aid Venezuela's development, Spain added it to the newly formed Viceroyalty of New Granada. Venezuela gained some relief from viceregal control when Spain put it under the rule of a captain-general (military governor) in 1777. It remained the Captaincy-General of Venezuela until the independence movement began in 1811.

On July 5, 1811, a national congress met in Caracas and declared Venezuela's independence from Spain. As a result, Venezuela became the first South American country to revolt against Spanish rule. Francisco de Miranda, a Venezuelan revolutionary known as El Precursor (the forerunner), assumed the role of dictator. Miranda was the "forerunner" to Simón Bolívar and others. Spain reacted harshly to the declaration. Spanish troops crushed the rebels and forced an armistice in July 1812. They captured Miranda and whisked him off to Cádiz in chains. Miranda spent the rest of his life in Spanish dungeons. He died four years later. Venezuela's struggle for independence was only starting, however. Simón Bolívar now took up the cause of freedom.

Simón Bolívar was born on July 24, 1783, in Caracas. His father was an aristocrat of Spanish descent. He died when Simón was only three years old. His mother died six years later, and Simón inherited a fortune. At age sixteen, young Bolívar's uncle sent him to Europe to complete his education.

In 1802, while living in Spain, Bolívar met and married Maria Teresa del Toro y Alaysa. She was the daughter of a Caracas-born nobleman. Maria died of yellow fever within a year of their arrival in Caracas. Filled with grief, Bolívar sailed off again on a European tour.

1717 — Spain founds the Viceroyalty of New Granada

1718 — New Granada becomes part of Venezuela

1777 — Captaincy-General of Venezuela is established

1811 — Venezuela declares independence from Spain

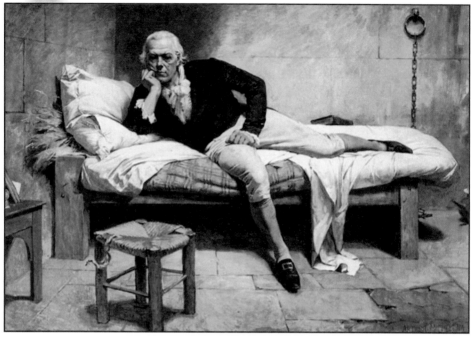

Miranda en La Carraca, Arturo Michelena's depiction of Francisco de Miranda's last days as a prisoner in Cádiz, Spain. Miranda preceded Simón Bolívar and was one of the first revolutionaries to fight against Spain.

Standing on the heights of Monte Sacro near Rome in 1805, he stared into the future. A vision of freedom seized his imagination. In a dramatic vow to a friend, Bolívar pledged to liberate all Hispanic South Americans: "I swear before you, my master, I swear before the God of the fathers, I swear by them, I swear by my honor that I will not let my arm or soul rest until I have broken the chains that oppress us because of the will of Spanish government."[1]

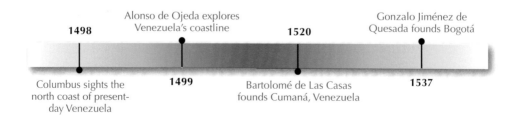

Alonso de Ojeda explores Venezuela's coastline

1498

Gonzalo Jiménez de Quesada founds Bogotá

1520

Columbus sights the north coast of present-day Venezuela

1499

Bartolomé de Las Casas founds Cumaná, Venezuela

1537

Bolívar felt determined to continue the revolution after the armistice of 1812. He fled to Cartagena in New Granada. While there, he wrote *El Manifiesto de Cartagena* (The Cartagena Manifesto). It was the first of his inspired political statements. "My purpose in writing this memorial is to spare New Granada the fate of Venezuela from the affliction it now suffers,"[2] Bolívar began.

Bolívar went on to urge the revolutionary forces to wipe out the power of Spain in Venezuela. In conclusion, he passionately scribed: "The honor of New Granada absolutely demands that we teach these audacious invaders a lesson, pursuing them to their last strongholds. . . . Rush forth to avenge death, to give life to the dying, succor to the oppressed, and freedom to all."[3] Bolívar himself rushed forth to meet the challenge of revolutionary leadership.

Simón Bolívar, known as El Libertador (The Liberator), led the revolutions against Spanish rule in New Granada. He ruled less successfully and died in Colombia in self-imposed exile.

Bolívar formed an expeditionary force to liberate Venezuela and launched a sweeping campaign against the Spaniards. After six fierce battles on the way to Caracas, he entered the city in victory on August 6,

1717

New Granada becomes part of Venezuela

1777

Venezuela declares independence from Spain

1718

Spain founds the Viceroyalty of New Granada

Captaincy-General of Venezuela is established

1811

1813. The people named him El Libertador (The Liberator). He assumed the role of dictator. But much fighting remained to be done.

In 1814, the Spaniards converted the *llaneros* into a fiercely effective cavalry of sorts. Under José Tomás Boves, a Spanish smuggler, the savage horsemen drove Bolívar out of Caracas. He fled again to New Granada. There, he took command of another force and captured Bogotá. Later, however, new defeats forced him to flee to Jamaica.

While in Jamaica, Bolívar penned the greatest political essay of his career, *La Carta de Jamaica* (The Letter from Jamaica). He wrote it as a letter to a British resident of the island, but he clearly meant it for a much larger audience. It described his grand view of separate and independent Spanish-speaking nations in Latin America, from Mexico to Argentina and Chile: "Success will crown our efforts because the destiny of [Latin] America is irrevocably fixed; the tie that bound her to Spain is severed, for it was nothing but an illusion binding together the two sides of that vast monarchy. What formerly united them now separates them."[4]

As he continued, Bolívar defined his concepts for individual Latin American constitutional republics. Using the government of Great Britain as a model, he envisioned a hereditary upper house, an elected lower house, and a president with a lifetime term. Critics point out the weakness of the latter provision. All in all, however, the Jamaica letter represents a masterwork of political thinking.

Near the end of his missive, Bolívar grandly asserted: "When we are at last strong, under the auspices of a liberal nation that lends us its protection, then we will cultivate in harmony the virtues and talents that lead to glory; then we will follow the majestic path toward abundant prosperity marked out by destiny for South America; then the arts

The Spaniards drive Bolívar out of Caracas

1813

1819

Simón Bolívar "The Liberator" reaches Caracas

1814

Bolívar becomes president of Venezuela; establishes republic of Gran Colombia

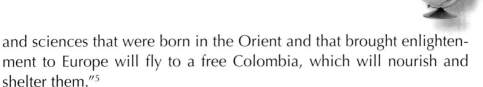
and sciences that were born in the Orient and that brought enlighten-ment to Europe will fly to a free Colombia, which will nourish and shelter them."[5]

In search of a "liberal nation," Bolívar turned to Haiti. The small island nation had freed itself from French rule when it declared inde-pendence in 1804. It now lent its sympathy to a fellow freedom seeker—along with money and guns. Bolívar organized another expe-ditionary force in Haiti.

In 1816, Bolívar landed in Venezuela and captured Angostura, a river port on the narrows of the Orinoco River (*Angostura* means "nar-rows" in Spanish; the city is now Ciudad Bolívar.). Bolívar set up his headquarters there. He assembled an army of foreign soldiers—mostly British and Irish—and *llaneros* who had shifted allegiance. In 1819, he completed his master plan for an assault on New Granada.

In one of the most daring operations in military history, Bolívar advanced up the Orinoco River with an army of 3,200 men. Marching some 700 miles through flood-swept plains and across the icy Andes range, he arrived in New Granada with only about a third of his origi-nal force. Reinforced by local volunteers, Bolívar engaged the royalist army at Boyacá on August 7, 1819. In a decisive battle, most of the royalists surrendered to Bolívar's forces. Bolívar marched into Bogotá three days later. His victory marked the turning point in the history of northern South America.

Bolívar then returned to Venezuela and headed the Congress of Angostura that established the republic of Gran (Grand) Colombia. Initially, the new republic consisted only of what are now Colombia and Venezuela. Bolívar became its first president on December 17, 1819. He continued to seek out and crush royalist forces, soundly

1821 — Panama joins the Republic of Gran Colombia

1822 — Ecuador joins the Republic of Gran Colombia

1830 — Bolívar dies; Colombia (including Panama), Ecuador, and Venezuela form separate nations

defeating the Spaniards at Carabobo in Venezuela on June 24, 1821. The Liberator had at last freed his homeland. Panama joined the republic that same year. Ecuador followed in 1822.

Bolívar's dream of forming a closely aligned union of South American states fell short of fulfillment. Power-hungry politicians and political infighting stretched the bonds that tied New Granada and Venezuela together. In 1824, Bolívar predicted a civil war if the

The Battle of Boyacá was one of the most decisive battles of Latin American independence. Simón Bolívar led the revolutionary army in defeating the Spanish forces in August 1819 at Boyacá in what is now Colombia. This painting, by J. W. Cañarete, is on display at the National Museum of Bogotá in Colombia.

The Spaniards drive
Bolívar out of Caracas

1813

1819

Simón Bolívar "The
Liberator" reaches Caracas

1814

Bolívar becomes president
of Venezuela; establishes
republic of Gran Colombia

two factions failed to heed his words. Both shunned his words, and civil war erupted in 1826. Bolívar assumed dictatorial powers in 1828. After a failed attempt on his life, he decided his presence was contributing to the violence and unrest. On May 8, 1830, he left Bogotá, intending to seek refuge in Europe.

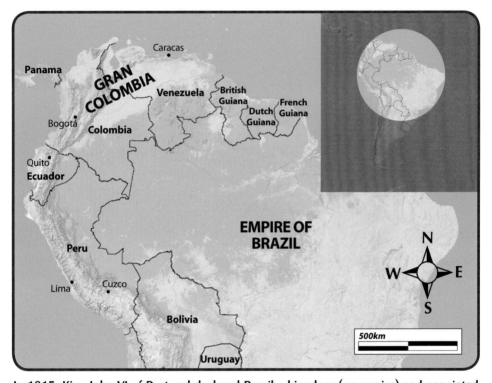

In 1815, King John VI of Portugal declared Brazil a kingdom (or empire) and appointed his son Pedro I as its emperor. Four years later, Simón Bolívar headed the Congress of Angostura and established the Republic of Great (or Gran) Colombia. The new republic covered an area that is now occupied by Colombia, Panama, Ecuador, and Venezuela.

1821

Panama joins the Republic of Gran Colombia

1822

Ecuador joins the Republic of Gran Colombia

1830

Bolívar dies; Colombia (including Panama), Ecuador, and Venezuela form separate nations

The meeting of José de San Martín (right) and Simón Bolívar (left) in Guayaquil, Ecuador, on July 25, 1822. San Martín deferred to Bolívar's leadership in the South American wars for independence against Spain. He spent the rest of his life in exile in Europe.

Ironically, Simón Bolívar—who had freed his nation from Spanish rule—died of tuberculosis in the home of a Spaniard near Santa Marta, Colombia, on December 17, 1830. Colombia (including Panama), Ecuador, and Venezuela split into three independent nations. The Republic of Gran Colombia disappeared into the mists of time.

Day of Glory

During the first six months of 1822, José de San Martín was still leading Peru's fight for independence. The great freedom fighter of southern South America had captured Peru's capital at Lima and its chief seaport at Callao. Still, much of the country remained in Spanish hands. San Martín called on Simón Bolívar, the great liberator, for help. The two heroic figures met at Quayaquil, Ecuador, on July 25, 1822.

History has not disclosed the details of their secret conversation. Scholars believe that San Martín wanted to establish a monarchy in Peru. Bolívar insisted on creating a Peruvian republic. Their differences remained unsettled. The ailing San Martín must have realized that Bolívar would not come to Peru unless he left. After helping to form a congress in Peru, San Martín told the lawmakers to seek Bolívar's help. He then retired to a self-imposed exile in Europe.

General Antonio José de Sucre

Bolívar arrived in Callao in September 1823. He assembled an army to confront Spanish troops in the mountains east of Lima. Advancing from his temporary capital at Trujillo, Bolívar joined his forces with those of General Antonio José de Sucre. With a combined army of some 9,000 men, they soundly defeated royalist forces in the Battle of Junin on August 6, 1824.

With victory in sight in Peru, the Colombian Congress recalled Bolívar to Gran Colombia. He dutifully obeyed the call, turning over the rest of the campaign to Sucre, his chief of staff and favorite general. Sucre led their army to a high plain near Ayacucho in Las Charcas (now Bolivia) to confront the enemy one last time.

On the morning of December 9, 1824, General Sucre addressed his troops: "Upon your efforts today depends the fate of South America. This shall be a day of glory that will crown your long struggles. Soldiers! Long live the Liberator! Long live Bolívar, the [savior] of Peru!"[6] In the ensuing Battle of Ayacucho, Sucre routed a much larger royalist army. Surrender terms called for the withdrawal of all Spanish forces from both Peru and neighboring Las Charcas. Sucre renamed Las Charcas as Bolivia in honor of Bolívar.

Viceroyalty
of New Granada

Guianas

Viceroyalty of Peru

Amazon River

Kingdom of
Brazil

Lima

La Paz

PACIFIC
OCEAN

Audiencia
of
Upper Peru

Rio de Janeiro

SOUTH
ATLANTIC
OCEAN

Viceroyalty
of La Plata

Buenos Aires

N
W   E
S

750km

An audiencia is a court of law that serves as an administrative representative of a district within a viceroyalty. The Audiencia of Upper Peru
roughly corresponds to today's Bolivia. It was also known as Las Charcas
and Chuquisaca.

Chapter 7

Las Charcas: Audiencia of Upper Peru

Las Charcas—or the Audiencia of Peru—corresponds roughly to present-day Bolivia. (*Las Charcas* means "the ponds" in Spanish.) It was also known as Upper Peru and Chuquisaca. Las Charcas included parts of today's Argentina, Chile, Peru, and Paraguay. Hernando Pizarro, half brother of Francisco Pizarro, conquered the region during the 1530s. Speaking about Inca resistance, he once boasted, "Ten Christians on horseback will suffice to subdue an army."[1] Spreading terror with snorting stallions and fire-spitting thunder-sticks, Hernando proved his boast.

The Spaniards founded the city of Choquechaca (an Indian name for "the pools") in 1538. When Las Charcas was established in 1559, it was attached to the Viceroyalty of Peru. It became the government seat of the audiencia. Over the years, it changed names three times and became known as the City of Four Names. When silver was discovered in nearby Porco, Choquechaca took the name of La Plata ("The Silver").

During the seventeenth century, the name of La Plata gave way to Chuquisaca. The name is a Spanish contraction of the city's original Indian name. In 1776, Las Charcas joined the newly formed Viceroyalty of La Plata. It remained a part of the new viceroyalty for another half century. Present-day Argentina, Uruguay, and Paraguay made up the rest of the viceroyalty. In December 1824, Sucre routed the Spaniards in the Battle of Ayacucho. Eight months later, another new nation emerged.

On August 6, 1825, a congress formed in Chuquisaca signed the Declaration of Independence. It changed the city's name to Sucre in honor of the hero of Ayacucho. Sucre, in turn, renamed Las Charcas as the Republic of Bolivia, for Simón Bolívar. He went on to become Bolivia's first president. The city named after him now serves as the constitutional capital of Bolivia. Sucre shares capital city status with the legislative and administrative seat at La Paz de Ayacucho (or simply La Paz).

Like most emerging nations, Bolivia experienced a full share of growing pains as it struggled to come of age. Its external problems began in 1835 when Bolivian dictator-president Andrés Santa Cruz invaded Peru. He hoped to unite Bolivia and Peru in a confederation and thereby expand his power base. Both Chile and Argentina opposed it. They feared such a

Battle of Ayacucho. In this battle, General Antonio José de Sucre routed a much larger royalist army. Surrender terms called for the withdrawal of all Spanish forces from both Peru and neighboring Las Charcas.

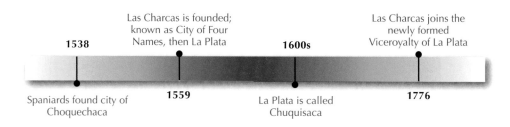

Las Charcas is founded; known as City of Four Names, then La Plata

1538

Las Charcas joins the newly formed Viceroyalty of La Plata

1600s

Spaniards found city of Choquechaca

1559

La Plata is called Chuquisaca

1776

union would upset the existing balance of power. Their opposition led to the War of the Peruvian-Bolivian Confederation, beginning on November 11, 1836. The conflict raged on for more than two years. On January 20, 1839, a strong Chilean army trounced confederation forces at Yungay, Chile, and the war ended. Santa Cruz was overthrown, terminating the confederation.

Two years later, Peruvian President Augustín Gamarra invaded Bolivia in an attempt to annex his neighbor. Bolivian forces smashed the invaders at the Battle of Ingavi on November 18, 1841. Gamarra was killed in the action. A peace treaty ended all efforts to unite the two countries. In 1884, the War of the Pacific with Chile (see chapter 5) ended Bolivia's territorial adventures in the nineteenth century. The war cost Bolivia the coastal region of Antofagasta, its only outlet to the sea.

Bolivia's internal and external turmoil continued throughout most of the 1900s. Bolivia settled a longstanding dispute with Brazil over Acre in 1903, ending several years of conflict. It ceded the region known for its rubber plantations to Brazil. In return, Bolivia received a sum of some $10 million. Revolution followed upon revolt. One dictator succeeded another. Political chaos, instability, and poverty ruled for much of the century. Tin from mountains once rich with silver constituted the nation's only important resource for export and trade.

In 1928, Bolivia entered into a land dispute with Paraguay. A disagreement arose over a wasteland of more than 100,000 square miles called Gran Chaco. Chaco Boreal is the main part of the region. It is located at the fork of the Paraguay and Pilcomayo Rivers. Bolivia pursued control of the region for two reasons: It wanted to gain access to

1824

Chuquisaca declares independence; name changes to Sucre; liberated Las Charcas becomes the Republic of Bolivia

1836–1839

Sucre routes the Spaniards in the Battle of Ayacucho

1825

War of the Peruvian-Bolivian Confederation is fought

the Atlantic, and it thought the region held large deposits of oil. In 1932, localized border clashes escalated into a full-blown war.

Paraguay attacked first. A formidable army led by General José Estigarribia captured Bolivia's Fortín (Fort) Bouquerón in September 1932. Late the following year, the Paraguayans launched a wide-scale successful offensive to control the region's scarce sources of drinking water. The Bolivian army consisted largely of highland Indians who were not used to the harsh climate. They died in droves and were gradually pushed back.

After bitter fighting around the outpost of Ballivián, Paraguayan forces controlled all of the Chaco. As they advanced into Bolivian territory, Bolivia sued for peace in 1935. A peace treaty signed in Buenos Aires in 1938 confirmed Paraguay's sovereignty over the Chaco region. Bolivia received rights to a narrow land corridor to the river port of Puerto Casado on the Paraguay River. The so-called Chaco War was the only major war fought among American countries in the twentieth century. It left some 100,000 people dead.

Bolivia's violent evolution continued in the aftermath of World War II as world demand for its mineral products fell off. In 1946, it entered a period of unemployment and inflation. Severe economic hardships developed as a result. Public dissatisfaction led to the Bolivian Revolt of 1946 in La Paz on July 17–21, 1946.

Rebellious workers, students, and soldiers staged violent demonstrations against the dictatorial regime of President Gualberto Villaroel. Their violence went unchecked by a sympathetic army. The five-day uprising ended when protestors seized Villaroel. They hanged him from a lamp post in front of the presidential palace. A temporary

	Chile crushes Peru and Bolivia in the War of the Pacific		Bolivian Revolt; President Villaroel is hanged
1841		**1932–1935**	
	1879–1884		**1946**
Bolivia stops Peruvian takeover in Battle of Ingavi		Bolivia loses Chaco War	

Bolivian soldiers marching through a fort they constructed during the Chaco War with Paraguay. Victory in the Chaco War confirmed Paraguay's sovereignty over the Chaco region. Bolivia received rights to a narrow land corridor to the Paraguay River.

Bolivian Guerrilla War begins

1952

1967

After Bolivian National Revolution, Paz Estenssoro is president

1966

Bolivian soldiers kill Ernesto "Che" Guevara, ending revolt

Rebellious workers, students, and soldiers staged violent demonstrations against Bolivian dictator General Gualberto Villaroel in 1946. They hanged him from a lamp post in front of the presidential palace.

Chile crushes Peru and Bolivia in the War of the Pacific

1841

1879–1884

1932–1935

Bolivian Revolt; President Villaroel is hanged

1946

Bolivia stops Peruvian takeover in Battle of Ingavi

Bolivia loses Chaco War

government was installed and order was restored. But order continued to remain fleeting in the lives of Bolivians.

On April 8–11, 1952, another popular revolt erupted in La Paz. Now known as the Bolivian National Revolution, it was one of South America's major revolutions. Armed workers, civilians, and peasants, along with the national police, overthrew a repressive ten-man military junta (HUN-tuh; government council). Victor Paz Estenssoro, the founder and leader of the previously outlawed National Revolutionary

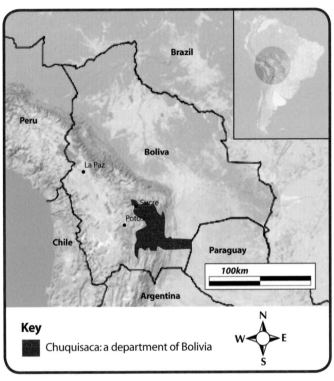

La Paz de Ayacucho (or simply La Paz) shares capital city status with Sucre. It serves as Bolivia's legislative and administrative seat.

Key

■ Chuquisaca: a department of Bolivia

1952

After Bolivian National Revolution, Paz Estenssoro is president

Bolivian Guerrilla War begins

1966

1967

Bolivian soldiers kill Ernesto "Che" Guevara, ending revolt

Movement, was recalled from exile in Argentina and installed as president.

Although ruthless to his political foes, Paz Estenssoro initiated major economic and political reforms. He nationalized the tin-mining industry and raised the wages of miners. Further, he liquidated the vast holdings of powerful landowners and redistributed acres to landless Indians. Under his guidance, Bolivia is said to have "suddenly broken loose from the chains of serfdom."[2] Bolivians, particularly the Indians, gained civil and political rights that would carry over to future regimes. But even the improvements made by Paz Estenssoro did not secure his position in a country prone to political instability. A military faction deposed him in 1964.

Two years later, Bolivia's harsh military regime provoked the Bolivian Guerrilla War. In November 1966, at La Paz, a balding, middle-aged man in a business suit stepped off an incoming airplane from São Paulo, Brazil. Customs officials cleared him as a Uruguayan agricultural researcher. In reality, he was Ernesto "Che" Guevara, the Argentine revolutionary famous for his leading role in the Cuban Revolution of 1956–1959.

Che wanted to make the Andes "the Sierra Maestra of South America."[3] (Fidel Castro launched the Cuban Revolution in Cuba's Sierra Maestra range.) But his attempt to jump-start a revolution in the Bolivian jungles with a few guerrillas failed.

In October 1967, Bolivian soldiers captured Che and shot him dead. History remembers him not so much for what he did as for how he did it. He dedicated his life to helping the helpless. Che left his legacy in a will for his children: "Be always capable of feeling, in the

Chile crushes Peru and Bolivia in the War of the Pacific

1841

1932–1935

Bolivian Revolt; President Villaroel is hanged

Bolivia stops Peruvian takeover in Battle of Ingavi

1879–1884

Bolivia loses Chaco War

1946

Peruvian President General Manuel A. Odria (right) and Bolivian President Doctor Victor Paz Estenssoro (left) watch the military parade during the Peruvian National Day festivities in 1955.

1952

After Bolivian National Revolution, Paz Estenssoro is president

Bolivian Guerrilla War begins

1966

1967

Bolivian soldiers kill Ernesto "Che" Guevara, ending revolt

Cuban Revolutionary legends Camilo Cienfuegos (left) and Ernesto Che Guevara (right) in Havana. Camilo died in a plane crash in October 1959 during a military mission. Guevara was executed in Bolivia in October 1967.

depths of your heart, any injustice committed against anyone any-where in the world."[4] At the dawn of a new millennium, Bolivia could do worse as it works hard to improve the quality of life for all its citizens.

La Paz

Located high in the Andes range of South America, La Paz is a city that scrapes the sky. It is nestled in the bowl-like canyon of the Choqueyapu River. As it expands, it climbs the surrounding hills to heights ranging from 9,842 to 13,451 feet (3,000 to 4,100 meters). The triple-peaked Illimani, Bolivia's highest peak at 21,201 feet (6,462 meters) above sea level, looks down on the city. Majestic and always snow-capped, it stands as a silent sentinel overlooking the world's loftiest capital city.

Like many cities in Bolivia, La Paz has undergone several name changes. It was founded in 1548 by Spanish conquistador Captain Alonso de Mendoza on the site of the Indian settlement of Chuquiago. The Indian name meant "gold field" because gold was washed there. Residents quickly named the settlement Nuestra Señora de La Paz, Spanish for "Our Lady of Peace." The name honored the restoration of peace after Gonzalo Pizarro and others rebelled against Blasco Nuñez Vela, the first viceroy of Peru, in 1548.

In 1825, after republican General Antonio José de Sucre defeated Spanish loyalist forces at Ayacucho, the city's name changed again to La Paz de Ayacucho, meaning The Peace of Ayacucho. Most of the world knows it now as simply La Paz.

In 1898, La Paz became the administrative capital of Bolivia. La Paz's enhanced status reflected the shift in Bolivia's economy from the played-out silver mines in the Potosí region to the burgeoning tin mines near Oruro. The legal capital remains in Sucre, however, resulting in a "shared capital" status for both cities.

As the most Indian nation of South America, Bolivia offers many historical and cultural attractions for today's traveler. In La Paz, the curious traveler will want to visit the Plaza Murillo, named for Bolivian independence hero General Pedro Domingo Murillo. A towering cathedral and the ornate Government Palace border the central plaza. Visitors can stroll narrow, cobblestoned streets to explore a variety of museums. The Museo de Oro (The Gold Museum), for example, exhibits pre-Columbian artifacts, and the Museo Nacional de Arqueologia features relics from Tiwanaku, Bolivia's premier archeological site.

Golfers can expect to hit their golf balls several meters farther than usual in the thin air of the world's highest golf course. On a more solemn note, motorists will want to use extra caution while navigating the hairpin bends along what is known as "the world's most dangerous road." The main road from La Paz to a region known as the Yungas claims hundreds of casualties each year along its fifty-mile stretch.

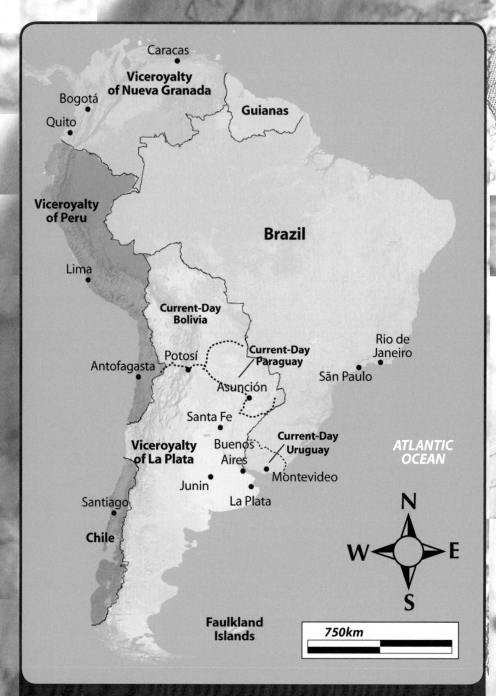

Caracas

**Viceroyalty
of Nueva Granada**

Bogotá

Guianas

Quito

**Viceroyalty
of Peru**

Brazil

Lima

**Current-Day
Bolivia**

Rio de
Janeiro

Potosí

**Current-Day
Paraguay**

Antofagasta

Asunción

Sãn Paulo

Santa Fe

**Viceroyalty
of La Plata**

**Current-Day
Uruguay**

Buenos
Aires

**ATLANTIC
OCEAN**

Montevideo

Junin

Santiago

La Plata

N

W   E

Chile

S

**Faulkland
Islands**

750km

Border disputes among developing South American countries were common. To establish their current borders, Bolivia fought with Chile, Paraguay, and Brazil; Paraguay clashed with Bolivia, Brazil, Uruguay, and Argentina; and Uruguay gained its independence from Brazil and fought with Paraguay. Brazil fought with all of them. Nation-building rarely comes without strife.

La Plata: River of Silver

Silver played an important role in the development of Bolivia. It also inspired the early exploration of the vast lands to the south. In 1516, Spanish explorer and mapmaker Juan Díaz de Solís sailed down the east coast of South America. While looking for a passage to the Spice Islands in the Far East, he found the estuary (ES-choo-air-ee; mouth) of the rivers known today as the Paraná and the Uruguay. When Solís went ashore to explore the area, unfriendly Charrúa Indians killed him and his party.

In 1527, Italian navigator Sebastian Cabot, sailing for Spain, entered the same estuary. Friendly Indians gave him silver trinkets and told him of a "White King" who ruled over a kingdom with mountains rich in silver. Thinking the estuary would lead him to a silvery kingdom, Cabot named it *Río de la Plata*—River of Silver. He sailed deep into the interior of what is now Argentina. But Cabot found neither king nor kingdom. He returned to Spain with silver trinkets and tales of a White King and silver mountains.

In 1535, King Charles I of Spain sent nobleman Pedro de Mendoza to found a city on the banks of the Río de la Plata. Mendoza established a crude clay-walled village in the clear Argentine air early the following year and called it *Santa María del Buen Aire*—Saint Mary of the Good Air. The air proved less than good for Mendoza. Disease struck him down, and he died at sea while trying to return to Spain.

Meanwhile, a group of Mendoza's men under Juan de Ayolas sailed up the Paraná to the junction of the Pilcomayo and Paraguay Rivers.

Italian navigator Sebastian Cabot explored the South American coastline for Spain. He was son of John Cabot, who claimed North America for England.

They built a wooden fort and named it *Nuestra Señora de las Asunción*—Our Lady of the Assumption. Ayolas continued upriver in search of silver. He found death instead at the hands of hostile Indians.

In 1541, the Buenos Aires settlers, under pressure from native attacks, abandoned their village and moved to Ayolas's settlement. Known as Asunción, it would later become the capital of Paraguay. In 1573, citizen-soldier Juan de Garay of Asunción founded Santa Fe as a port of call some six hundred miles down the river from Asunción. Seven years later, he reestablished Mendoza's original settlement, which is known today as Buenos Aires. In 1620, Spain attached its territories in southeastern South America to the Viceroyalty of Peru.

Since early explorers found no gold or silver in the La Plata region, the lower half of South America developed slowly. Portugal began to take an interest in the region in 1680. It established Nova Colonia de Sacramento (now Colonia) across the La Plata estuary from Buenos Aires. The area of rolling plains on the river's east bank was called Banda Oriental. It stayed unsettled for years because of resistance from

Sebastian Cabot sails down Río de la Plata into what is now Argentina

1516   1535

Juan de Garay of Asunción founds Santa Fe

1580

Juan Díaz de Solís explores Paraná and Uruguay rivers

1527

Santa María del Buen Aire and Nuestra Señora de las Asunción are founded

1573

Santa María del Buen Aire becomes Buenos Ares

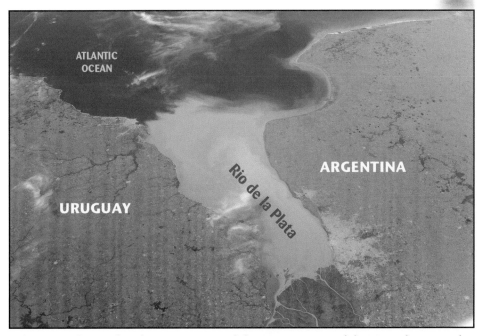

ATLANTIC
OCEAN

URUGUAY

Río de la Plata

ARGENTINA

Sebastian Cabot, sailing for Spain, entered the great estuary of the rivers known today as the Paraná and the Uruguay. Thinking the estuary would lead him to a silvery kingdom, Cabot named it Río de la Plata—River of Silver.

its fierce Charrúa Indian inhabitants. They preferred death to surrender and suppression.

In 1726, in an effort to check Portuguese expansion in the region, Spain founded Montevideo at the entrance to the Río de la Plata. Montevideo would later serve as the capital of Uruguay. To further curb Portuguese influence, Spain also encouraged the growth of Buenos

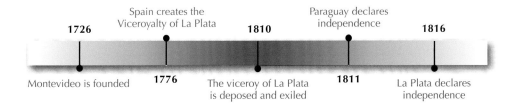

Spain creates the
Viceroyalty of La Plata

Paraguay declares
independence

1726   1810   1816

Montevideo is founded   1776   The viceroy of La Plata   1811   La Plata declares
is deposed and exiled   independence

Monument of Juan de Garay in Buenos Aires. Garay founded Santa Fe as a port of call some six hundred miles downriver from Asunción. In 1580, he reestablished the estuary settlement that is known today as Buenos Aires.

Aires. Spanish and Portuguese troops spent much of the 1700s battling for control of the Uruguay region.

In 1776, Spain created the Viceroyalty of La Plata (or Buenos Aires). It was the last of its four viceroyalties in the Americas. It comprised the future nations of Argentina, Paraguay, Uruguay, and Bolivia. Buenos Aires served as the new seat of government.

Spain figured that a new viceroyalty would enable it to take better control of its southeastern territories. Spain felt pressured by the Portuguese presence on the north shore of the La Plata. Further, Great Britain was threatening to take possession of the Spanish-held Islas Malvinas (Falkland Islands).

During the early 1800s, discontent with Spanish rule began to sweep across Latin America like a pampa (prairie) stampede. The great independence movement was about to turn the map of Latin America into a mosaic of free and separate nations.

Sebastian Cabot sails down Río de la Plata into what is now Argentina

1516

1535

Juan de Garay of Asunción founds Santa Fe

1580

Juan Díaz de Solís explores Paraná and Uruguay rivers

1527

Santa María del Buen Aire and Nuestra Señora de las Asunción are founded

1573

Santa María del Buen Aire becomes Buenos Ares

Buenos Aires, which flourished as the government seat of La Plata, became the center of the revolutionary movement in the south. The city's upper-class Creoles (persons of Spanish descent born in the New World) took the lead in the great rebellion. On May 25, 1810, in an open town meeting called a *cabildo abierto* (kuh-BEEL-doh ah-bee-AIR-toh), they deposed and exiled the viceroy of La Plata. Then they established an independent government to administer the viceroyalty. In 1811, the people of Asunción overthrew the Spanish governor and declared their independence as the new nation of Paraguay. Buenos Aires and Asunción had taken the first steps toward independence in the lower regions of South America.

Argentine General José de San Martín took the next step. At his urging, representatives of the provinces met at the Congress of Tucumán to discuss how to achieve future stability in the region. According to a Latin American study, "San Martín chose the side of an outright declaration of independence from Spain."[1] On July 9, 1816, the congress officially declared La Plata's independence. The Argentine provinces banded together as the United Provinces of the Río de la Plata. The outlying provinces opposed the union, however, and went their separate ways. With San Martín leading the way, the revolution moved ahead.

San Martín was a career soldier who had fought against Napoleon in Spain. He worked closely with Chilean patriot Bernardo O'Higgins to develop a Continental Plan to free South America from Spanish control. The plan called for him to cross the Andes, to liberate Chile, and ultimately to seize the Spanish stronghold of Lima in the Viceroyalty of Peru. In February 1817, San Martín surprised and defeated Spanish forces just north of Santiago, Chile, at the Battle of Chacabuco.

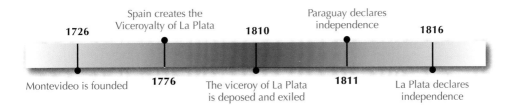

| 1726 | Spain creates the Viceroyalty of La Plata | 1810 | Paraguay declares independence | 1816 |

Montevideo is founded   1776   The viceroy of La Plata is deposed and exiled   1811   La Plata declares independence

In February 1817, General José de San Martín surprised and defeated Spanish forces just north of Santiago, Chile, in the Battle of Chacabuco. The battle served as a prelude to the decisive battle for Chilean independence at the Maipú River two months later.

Argentine-Chilean forces finalized their hold on Chile with a victory at the Battle of Maipú in April 1818.

In August 1820, San Martín mounted a naval assault on Peru. He entered Lima in July 1821. After a brief stay in Peru, he traveled to Guayaquil, Ecuador, to meet with fellow liberator Simón Bolívar. After two days of talks, presumably about continuing the military campaign, the general withdrew from Guayaquil under mysterious circumstances.

1817

Chile wins independence

1821

Estado Oriental gains independence

Chilean rebels defeat the Spanish in the Battle of Chacabuco

1818

Mexico and Central American states win independence; Estado Oriental (Eastern State) is formed

1828

In the April 1818 Battle of Maipú, General José de San Martín led some 9,000 Argentine-Chilean rebels in a stunning victory of about 6,000 Spanish Royalists led by General Manuel Osorio. The victory assured Chile's independence.

With battles still to be won, San Martín left the rest of the fighting to Bolívar. Later, from voluntary retirement in France, the old warrior continued to give "moral support to the defenders of American sovereignty."[2] San Martín died peacefully in Boulonge-sur-Mer, France, on August 17, 1850.

Meanwhile, across the Río de la Plata, Montevideo and the surrounding area formed the separate state of Estado Oriental (Eastern

In War of the Triple Alliance, Argentina, Brazil, and Uruguay defeat Paraguay

Augusto Pinochet heads a military government in Chile

1830

1946–1955

Uruguay adopts its first constitution

1865–1870

Juan Perón is president of Argentina

1974–1990

José de San Martín's remains are entombed in a mausoleum apart from the Buenos Aires Metropolitan Church, the city's main Catholic church. The tomb is separated from the main body of the cathedral because San Martín was believed to be a Freemason and therefore ineligible for burial in the cathedral proper.

State). After years of resisting the rule of Spain, Buenos Aires, and Portuguese Brazil, Estado Oriental gained its hard-fought independence in 1828. The new nation of Uruguay adopted its first constitution two years later. By then, Bolivia had gained its freedom (see chapter 7). Spain's once-vast empire in South America ceased to exist.

Most South American nations adopted a republican form of government. In the twentieth century, they all joined the United Nations after World War II. And most joined the Organization of American States (OAS) in 1948. The OAS membership now consists of the United States and all the independent countries of Latin America.

Along their paths to the present, all South American nations experienced border disputes. In the War of the Triple Alliance (1865–1870), for example, Argentina, Brazil, and Uruguay defeated Paraguay to firmly establish the borders of all four countries.

Citizens of every nation endured social and economic inequalities, which led inevitably to iron-fisted dictators and popular revolts.

1817

Chile wins independence

1821

Estado Oriental gains independence

Chilean rebels defeat the Spanish in the Battle of Chacabuco

1818

Mexico and Central American states win independence; Estado Oriental (Eastern State) is formed

1828

Augusto Pinochet of Chile and Juan Perón in Argentina typify the popular image of a tyrannical ruler.

Augusto Pinochet headed a military government in Chile and ruled harshly for sixteen years. Free elections finally unseated him in 1990, but not before the have-nots of Chile suffered through years of high inflation and acute hardship.

Juan Perón helped to overthrow a weak Argentine government in 1943 and was elected president three years later. He won the hearts of workers by showering them with essential benefits. At the same time, however, he drastically restricted their civil rights. His policies vacillated politically from left to

Augusto Pinochet, a tyrannical ruler, headed a military government in Chile. He ruled harshly for sixteen years.

right and back again. Argentines eventually developed a love-hate relationship with him and overthrew him in 1955.

And in Argentina there was also Evita.

Eva Perón, the wife and chief aide of Juan Perón, understood her people and watched over them like a Madonna. Her adoring Argentines called her "Evita"—little Eva. She touched their hearts and felt

In War of the Triple Alliance, Argentina, Brazil, and Uruguay defeat Paraguay

1830

Augusto Pinochet heads a military government in Chile

1946–1955

Uruguay adopts its first constitution

1865–1870

Juan Perón is president of Argentina

1974–1990

Argentine president Juan Perón (left), his wife the former actress Eva Perón, and a close friend, Colonel Domingo Mercante. They sit in the Peróns' home in Olivos, Buenos Aires, in 1950. Eva, known affectionately as Evita, fought tirelessly for women's voting rights, campaigned to improve the lot of workers, and built hospitals and schools.

their pain. "Everything is melodramatic in the lives of the humble," she once said. "Because the poor don't invent sorrow, they bear it."[3]

Today, as the still-developing nations of Latin America strive to improve their standard of living, the echoing cries of Evita still inspire hope and banish sorrow.

Evita

Her parents named her María Eva Duarte. Argentines came to love her—or hate her—as Evita. During her short lifespan, she became the most powerful woman in the history of Argentina—or, perhaps, of the entire world. Her early death at the age of thirty-three initiated one of the largest displays of public mourning the world has ever witnessed.

Born to a poor family in 1919 in Los Toldos, in the province of Buenos Aires, she was the only girl among four brothers. Her father died when she was only six or seven. Her mother ran a boardinghouse. At age sixteen, Evita left school and went to Buenos Aires to pursue her dream of becoming an actress. With only a modest talent, she nonetheless won some fame as an actress. Destiny of another sort waited in the wings for her.

In 1945, Evita married Colonel Juan Perón, an official in Argentina's new military government. When Juan ran for president the following year, Evita campaigned hard for him. She appealed particularly to the workers who shared her humble origins. She affectionately called them *los descamisados* (los des-kahm-ee-SAH-dos; "the shirtless ones"), and they adored her. Her husband won the election, and Evita served as an unofficial secretary of labor in his administration.

Evita and Juan Perón, October 1951

Evita fought tirelessly for women's voting rights, campaigned to improve the lot of workers, built hospitals and schools to fight disease and educate the masses, and much more. She became the center of power, the voice, and the soul of the Perón movement in Argentina. For all those things, rivals in the military government hated her almost as much as her beloved descamisados loved her.

After her death from cancer on July 26, 1952, her adoring masses held a vigil that lasted for fourteen days. To them, she was a saint. By century's end, she had become the subject of innumerable articles, books, stage plays, and movies, as well as the object of endless controversy. This is the legacy of the woman who preferred to be called Evita, if the name "could be used to quell a pain or to weep a tear."[4]

1484	Columbus plans his grand "Enterprise of the Indies."
1492	Columbus discovers the New World.
1493	Columbus begins his second voyage.
1494	The Treaty of Tordesillas is signed.
1498	On third voyage, Columbus sights the north coast of present-day Venezuela and explores the South American coastline.
1499	Alonso de Ojeda explores Venezuela's coastline.
1500	Pedro Álvares Cabral discovers Brazil.
1502	On fourth voyage, Columbus lands on the Isthmus of Panama.
1506	Columbus dies in Valladolid, Spain.
1510	Vasco Núñez de Balboa founds Spanish colony of Darién.
1511	Velásquez conquers and colonizes Cuba.
1513	Vasco Núñez de Balboa discovers the Pacific Ocean.
1516	Juan Díaz de Solís discovers the estuary later named Río de la Plata by Sebastian Cabot (1527).
1517	Córdoba explores what is now Mexico.
1518	Grijalba calls the region "New Spain."
1519	Hernán Cortés lands near Veracruz, Mexico. He attacks the Aztecs.
1520	Bartolomé de Las Casas founds the first European settlement in South America at Cumaná, Venezuela.
1521	The Aztecs surrender to Cortés. He builds Mexico City.
1527	Sebastian Cabot sails down Río de la Plata into what is now Argentina.
1530	Portuguese settlers arrive in Brazil; Francisco Pizarro lands in Peru.
1532–1533	Pizarro conquers the Incas.
1535	Spain establishes the Viceroyalty of New Spain; Pizarro founds his capital at Lima, Peru; Diego de Almagro

	explores Chile; Santa María del Buen Aire and Nuestra Señora de las Asunción are founded.
1537	Gonzalo Jiménez de Quesada founds the city of Bogotá.
1538	Spaniards found city of Choquechaca.
1540	Francisco Vásquez de Coronado leads an expedition in search of the Seven Cities of Cibola.
1542	Spain founds the Viceroyalty of Peru; Francisco de Orellana navigates the length of the Amazon River.
1544	Spain establishes the Kingdom of Guatemala.
1550	French establish a colony at Guanabara Bay, Brazil.
1559	Las Charcas (Audiencia of Upper Peru) is founded; known as City of Four Names, then La Plata.
1567	The Portuguese found São Sebastião Rio de Janeiro.
1573	Juan de Garay of Asunción founds Santa Fe.
1580	Santa María del Buen Aire becomes Buenos Ares.
1580	Portugal becomes a Spanish domain and remains so until 1640.
1593	Spain claims the Guiana region.
1595	Sir Walter Raleigh leads first expedition to Guiana.
1600s	La Plata is called Chuquisaca.
1617	Sir Walter Raleigh mounts second expedition to Guiana.
1621	Dutch settlers arrive in Guiana.
1624	French settle in Guiana.
1651	English planters arrive in Guiana.
1667	Treaty of Breda establishes Dutch Guiana and French Guiana.
1717	Spain founds the Viceroyalty of New Granada.
1718	New Granada becomes part of Venezuela.
1726	Montevideo is founded at the entrance to the Río de la Plata.
1750	Treaty of Madrid is signed.
1776	Spain creates the Viceroyalty of Rio de la Plata. Guatemala City is built. Las Charcas joins newly formed Viceroyalty of La Plata.

1777	Captaincy-General of Venezuela is established.
1783	Simón Bolívar is born in Caracas, Venezuela.
1810	The viceroy of La Plata is deposed and exiled.
1811	Venezuela declares independence from Spain; Paraguay proclaims its independence.
1813	Simón Bolívar "The Liberator" reaches Caracas.
1814	The Spaniards drive Bolívar out of Caracas.
1815	Portugal declares Brazil a kingdom.
1816	Congress of Tucumán declares La Plata's independence.
1817	Chilean rebels defeat the Spanish army in the Battle of Chacabuco.
1818	Chilean patriots defeat Spanish forces in the Battle of Maipú; Chile wins its independence.
1819	Bolívar becomes president of Venuzuela; establishes republic of Gran Colombia.
1821	Mexico and Central American states win independence from Spain; Panama joins the Republic of Gran Colombia. Estado Oriental (Eastern State) is formed.
1822	Brazil proclaims its independence; Ecuador joins the Republic of Gran Colombia; José de San Martín and Simón Bolívar meet at Quayaquil, Ecuador.
1823	United Provinces of Central America is formed.
1824	Peruvian rebels defeat Spanish royalists in the Battles of Junin and Ayacucho; Peru gains its independence from Spain.
1825	Chuquisaca declares independence; name changes to Sucre; liberated Las Charcas becomes the Republic of Bolivia.
1828	Estado Oriental gains independence.
1830	Bolívar dies near Santa Marta, Colombia; Colombia (including Panama), Ecuador, and Venezuela form separate nations. Uruguay adopts its first constitution.
1831	Great Britain establishes British Guiana.
1836	Mexico loses northern lands to Texas in its war for independence; War of the Peruvian-Bolivian Confederation begins and lasts until 1839.

Timeline

1841	Central American states become separate and independent republics; Bolivia defeats Peru in the Battle of Ingavi.
1846–1848	United States defeats Mexico in the Mexican-American War.
1852	France establishes a penal colony on Devil's Island.
1861	Spain, Great Britain, and France invade Mexico.
1862	Mexico defeats France on May 5 (Cinco de Mayo).
1864	Mexican conservatives overthrow the regime of Benito Juárez.
1865–1870	In War of the Triple Alliance, Argentina, Brazil, and Uruguay defeat Paraguay.
1867	Mexicans topple Emperor Maximilian and execute him.
1877	After Battle of Tecoac, Diaz becomes dictator-president.
1879–1884	Chile crushes Peru and Bolivia in the War of the Pacific.
1889	Brazilian republic is founded.
1910–1920	Mexican Revolution fosters the creation of a liberal constitution; Alvaro Obregón becomes elected president.
1932–1935	Bolivia loses most of the Chaco region to Paraguay in the Chaco War.
1938	France abolishes its penal colonies.
1942	Peru defines its present boundaries.
1946	French Guiana becomes a French overseas *départmente* (department); Bolivian Revolt; Juan Perón is elected president of Argentina.
1952	Bolivian citizens gain civil and political rights in the Bolivian National Revolution.
1960	Brazil's seat of government is moved from Rio de Janeiro to Brasilia.
1966	Guyana (British Guiana) is established as an independent nation; Bolivian Guerrilla War begins but lasts only one year.
1967	Bolivian soldiers kill Ernesto "Che" Guevara, ending revolt.
1975	Dutch Guiana achieves independence as the new nation of Suriname.
1985	Brazil returns to civilian rule.
1990	Augusto Pinochet is unseated as president of Chile by free elections after sixteen years.

Timeline

2000	Police and soldiers clash with 700 farmers squatting on a 25,000-acre ranch in Paraguay to demand land reform. About one percent of Paraguay's five million people own 77 percent of its land.
2001	Argentine Senate passes a law that fixes the Argentine peso to the European euro as well as to the U.S. dollar. 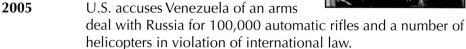
2002	UN World Food Program conducts an emergency operation to help Guatemalan children at risk of malnutrition resulting from the previous year's drought.
2003	Brazilian government offers workers a 20 percent pay raise to offset inflation.
2004	Cuban President Fidel Castro leads tens of thousands in a rally through the streets of Havana to protest recent tougher U.S. sanctions imposed on Cuba.
2005	U.S. accuses Venezuela of an arms deal with Russia for 100,000 automatic rifles and a number of helicopters in violation of international law.
2006	Mexico's Federal Electoral Tribunal rules that Felipe Calderón won the July presidential elections; Calderón takes office in December for a six-year term.
2007	U.S. President George W. Bush and Mrs. Bush tour Brazil, Uruguay, Colombia, Guatemala, and Mexico to underscore the commitment of the United States to the Western Hemisphere. Their trip highlights a common agenda to advance freedom, prosperity, and social justice, as well as health, education, and economic opportunity. 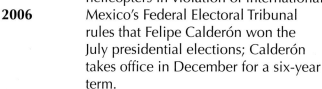

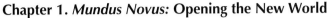
Chapter 1. *Mundus Novus:* Opening the New World

1. Michael Foss, *Undreamed Shores: England's Wasted Empire in America* (London: Phoenix Press, 2000), p. 16.

2. Ibid.

3. Peter Kemp (editor), *The Oxford Companion to Ships and the Sea* (New York: Oxford University Press, 1988), p. 183.

4. James R. McGovern, "Columbus, a Renaissance Man," in *The World of Columbus*, edited by James R. McGovern (Macon, GA: Mercer University Press, 1992), p. 16.

Chapter 2. New Spain: The Coming of the Conquistadors

1. Angus Konstam, *Historical Atlas of Exploration 1492–1600* (New York: Checkmark Books, 2000), p. 97.

2. Paolo Novaresio, *The Explorers: From the Ancient World to the Present* (New York: Stewart, Tabori & Chang, 1996), p. 130.

3. Fabienne Rousso-Lenoir, *America Latina* (New York: Assouline Publishing, 2002), p. 178.

4. Ibid., p. 174.

Chapter 3. Kingdom of Brazil: Island of the True Cross

1. Richard E. Bohlander (editor), *World Explorers and Discoverers* (New York: Da Capo Press, 1998), p. 89.

2. John Charles Chasteen, *Born in Blood and Fire: A Concise History of Latin America* (New York: W. W. Norton & Company, 2001), p. 77.

3. Anne Merriman Peck, *The Pageant of South American History* (Third edition. New York: David McKay Company, 1965), p. 319.

4. Fabienne Rousso-Lenoir, *America Latina* (New York: Assouline Publishing, 2002), p. 220.

5. Dan Rosenberg, "History of Carnival in Brazil," http://www.afropop.org/multi/feature/ID/33/

Chapter 4. Guiana: The Search for El Dorado

1. Jane Edmonds (editor), *Oxford Atlas of Exploration* (New York: Oxford University Press, 1997), pp. 100–101.

2. Richard E. Bohlander (editor), *World Explorers and Discoverers* (New York: Da Capo Press, 1998), p. 331.

3. Charles Nicholl, *The Creature in the Map: A Journey to El Dorado* (New York: William Morrow and Company, 1995), p. 194.

Chapter 5. Inca Gold: Viceroyalty of Peru

1. Anne Merriman Peck, *The Pageant of South American History*, third edition (New York: David McKay Company, 1965), p. 69.

2. Jane Edmonds (editor), *Oxford Atlas of Exploration* (New York: Oxford University Press, 1997), p. 99.

Chapter 6. Gran Colombia: Simón Bolívar and the Revolt against Spain

1. Fabienne Rousso-Lenoir, *America Latina* (New York: Assouline Publishing, 2002), p. 170.

2. Simón Bolívar, *El Libertador: Writings of Simón Bolívar*, translated from the Spanish by Frederick H. Fornoff and edited with an introduction and notes by David Bushnell (New York: Oxford University Press, 2003), p. 3.

3. Ibid., pp. 10, 11.

4. Ibid., p. 13.

5. Ibid., p. 30.

6. Anne Merriman Peck, *The Pageant of South American History*, third edition (New York: David McKay Company, 1965), p. 276.

Chapter 7. Las Charcas: Audiencia of Upper Peru

1. Anne Merriman Peck, *The Pageant of South American History*, third edition (New York: David McKay Company, 1965), p. 77.

2. George C. Kohn, *Dictionary of Wars* (New York: Facts On File, 1986), p. 61.

3. John Charles Chasteen, *Born in Blood and Fire: A Concise History of Latin America* (New York: W. W. Norton & Company, 2001), p. 266.

4. Fabienne Rousso-Lenoir, *America Latina* (New York: Assouline Publishing, 2002), p. 186.

Chapter 8. La Plata: River of Silver

1. Latin American Studies: *José de San Martín—The Knight of the Andes* http://www.latinamericanstudies.org/argentina/sanmartin-knight.htm

2. Ibid.

3. Fabienne Rousso-Lenoir, *America Latina* (New York: Assouline Publishing, 2002), p. 195.

4. *Mi Buenos Aires Querido* (My Dear Buenos Aires): Eva Perón http://www.mibsasquerido.com.ar/wcelebrities02.htm

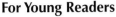

Further Reading

For Young Readers

Dougherty, Terri. *Argentina*. Modern Nations of the World Series. Farmington Hills, MI: Thomson Gale, 2003.

Kohn, George C. *Dictionary of Wars*. New York: Checkmark Books, 2006.

Lopata, Peg. *Colombia*. Modern Nations of the World Series. Farmington Hills, MI: Thomson Gale, 2004.

Machado, Ana Maria. *Latin America*. Exploration Into Series. New York: Chelsea House Publishers, 2000.

Pelusey, Michael, and Jane Pelusey. *South America*. Continent Series. New York: Chelsea House Publishers, 2004.

Salentiny, Fernand. *Encyclopedia of World Explorers: From Armstrong to Shackleton*. Edited by Werner Waldmann. London: Dumont monte, 2003.

Schaffer, David. *Discovering South America's Land, People, and Wildlife*. Continents of the World Series. Berkeley Heights, NJ: Enslow Publishers, 2004.

Works Consulted

Bedini, Silvio A. *Christopher Columbus and the Age of Exploration: An Encyclopedia*. New York: Da Capo Press, 1998.

Bohlander, Richard E. (editor). *World Explorers and Discoverers*. New York: Da Capo Press, 1998.

Bolívar, Simón. *El Libertador: Writings of Simón Bolívar*. Translated from the Spanish by Frederick H. Fornoff and edited with an introduction and notes by David Bushnell. New York: Oxford University Press, 2003.

Chasteen, John Charles. *Born in Blood and Fire: A Concise History of Latin America*. New York: W. W. Norton & Company, 2001.

Daniels, Patricia S., and Stephen G. Hyslop. *Almanac of World History*. Washington, DC: National Geographic Society, 2003.

Edmonds, Jane (editor). *Oxford Atlas of Exploration*. New York: Oxford University Press, 1997.

Foss, Michael. *Undreamed Shores: England's Wasted Empire in America*. London: Phoenix Press, 2000.

Kemp, Peter, ed. *The Oxford Companion to Ships and the Sea*. New York: Oxford University Press, 1988.

Konstam, Angus. *Historical Atlas of Exploration 1492–1600*. New York: Checkmark Books, 2000.

McGovern, James R. (editor). *The World of Columbus*. Macon, GA: Mercer University Press, 1992.

Nicholl, Charles. *The Creature in the Map: A Journey to El Dorado*. New York: William Morrow and Company, 1995.

Novaresio, Paolo. *The Explorers: From the Ancient World to the Present*. New York: Stewart, Tabori & Chang, 1996.

Nugent, David. *Modernity at the Edge of Empire: State, Individual, and Nation in the Northern Peruvian Andes, 1885–1935*. Stanford, CA: Stanford University Press, 1997.

Peck, Anne Merriman. *The Pageant of South American History*. Third edition. New York: David McKay Company, 1965.

Rousso-Lenoir, Fabienne. *America Latina*. New York: Assouline Publishing, 2002.

Voss, Stuart F. *Latin America in the Middle Period 1750–1929*. Wilmington, DE: Scholarly Resources, 2002.

Williamson, Edwin. *The Penguin History of Latin America*. New York: Penguin Books, 1992.

On the Internet

Afropop Worldwide: *History of Carnival in Brazil*
    http://www.afropop,org/multi/feature/ID/33/
Brazil: History of Brazil
    http://www.v-brazil.com/information/
CNN.com: Brazil readies for commercial carnival
    http://edition.cnn.com/2006/TRAVEL/02/13/brazil.trade/index.html
Latin American Studies: *José de San Martín — The Knight of the Andes*
    http://www.latinamericanstudies.org/argentina/sanmartin-knight.htm
Mi Buenos Aires Querido (My Dear Buenos Aires): Eva Perón
    http://www.mibsasquerido.com.ar/wcelebrities02.htm
United Fruit Company
    http://www.mayaparadise.com/ufc1e.htm

Amerindian (aa-mer-IN-dee-an)—American Indian; any of the native peoples of the Western Hemisphere, except for Eskimos and Aleuts.

audiencia (od-ee-EN-see-ah)—A court of law; administrative representative of a district within a viceroyalty.

banana republic—Latin American country with a banana-based economy; by extension, any country with an economy based on a single commodity.

cabildo abierto (kuh-BEEL-doh ah-bee-AIR-toh)—Spanish for "open town meeting."

El Dorado (ell-duh-RAH-doh)—Spanish for "the golden man"; a city or country of fabulous riches held by 16th-century explorers to exist in South America; a place of great wealth or opportunity.

estuary (ES-choo-air-ee)—A water passage where the tide meets a river current; the seaward mouth of a river.

fidalgo (fee-DAHL-go)—Portuguese for "nobleman."

Hispaniola (his-pan-YOH-la)—Island of the West Indies, currently divided between Haiti and the Dominican Republic.

Latin America—Broadly, all the nations south of the United States in the Western Hemisphere; all Spanish-speaking nations in the Western Hemisphere.

llano (LAH-noh)—Spanish for "grassy plain."

llanero (lah-NAIR-oh)—Spanish for "plainsman" or "cowboy."

los descamisados (los des-kahm-ee-SAH-dos)—Spanish for "the shirtless ones," these were laborers in Argentina.

Mundus Novus (MOON-dus NO-vus)—Latin for "New World."

province (PRAH-vins)—a district or region of a country.

Spanish Main—The mainland coast of the Spanish Empire around the Caribbean Sea and the Gulf of Mexico.

Tenochtitlán (tay-notch-teet-LAN)—Capital of the Aztec Empire.

Tordesillas (tor-day-SEEL-yas)—A little town in central Spain; site of the signing of the treaty by the same name in 1494.

viceroyalty (VISE-roi-il-tee)—The area ruled by a viceroy, a deputy of a king or sovereign; also the office or term of a viceroy.

Index

Index

Index

About the Author

Earle Rice Jr. is a former senior design engineer and technical writer in the aerospace, electronic-defense, and nuclear industries. He has devoted full time to his writing since 1993 and is the author of more than fifty published books. Earle is listed in *Who's Who in America* and is a member of the Society of Children's Book Writers and Illustrators; the League of World War I Aviation Historians and its UK-based sister organization, Cross & Cockade International; the United States Naval Institute; the Air Force Association; and the Disabled American Veterans.